GHOST TRAILS OF THE YORKSHIRE DALES

by
CLIVE KRISTEN

Casdec Ltd

Ghost Trails of the Yorkshire Dales

Dedication

To Ted Bottomley of Crosshills for kindling a love of the outdoors, and to my Mum for buying a cottage in the Yorkshire Dales.

Ghost Trails of the Yorkshire Dales

Published by Casdec Ltd
22 Harraton Terrace
Birtley
Chester-le-Street
Co Durham
DH3 2QG

Tel: (091) 410 5556
Fax: (091) 410 0229

Written by Clive Kristen

First Published June 1994

© Casdec June 1994

All rights reserved. No part of this publication may be reproduced, stored, in a retrieval system or transmitted in any form or by any means, electronic, mechanical, photocopying, recording or otherwise, without prior consent of the copyright owners.

Views and opinions expressed in this book are those of the author and not to be attributed to the publishers.

ISBN 0 907595 89 8

Author's Note

Dear Ghosthunter,

This book contains six 'tour and explore' trails linked by supernatural themes.

These trails have been constructed to take best advantage of the great natural beauty of the region, and to bring to life the rich historical and cultural heritage of the Yorkshire Dales.

The 'touring times' suggested for each trail are based on a fairly brisk schedule. For those who prefer relaxed ghosthunting each trail can be conveniently broken down into sections. Some of the longer trails could be easily extended to take three or four days. The Trail Guides provided with each section are intended only to help make sense of the text : they are not to scale and should not be regarded as an adequate substitute for a good map.

Whilst every effort has been made to produce accurate historical and topographical detail, the reader will understand that no area of human consciousness is more prone to misinterpretation, confusion, and even dishonesty than the supernatural.

In an attempt to make sense of this dilemma the book tries to balance traditional accounts of supernatural phenomena, archive and historical material, with the common sense of local knowledge. When it has been necessary to select one version of a story from several, contemporary and local accounts have taken precedence.

The historical notes are intended to fill out detail where it has not been appropriate to do so within the main body the the text. This final section also corrects a measure of imbalance.

Ghost Trails of the Yorkshire Dales

I am indebted to archivists and librarians in Britain and abroad without whose patience and perseverance this would have been a very much slimmer volume. An acknowledgement list included at the end of the book.

I am also most greatful to all those who have written to my publisher, or who have taken part in 'supernatural' phone-ins on local radio, or have responded directly to newspaper features. I also wish to record a debt of gratitude to those who have given permission for their stories to be retold.

Once again my greatest debt is to my wife, Maureen, for her encouragement, ghosthunting and mapmaking skills, and infinite patience.

Clive Kristen
June 1994

The Writer

Former teacher and lecturer, CLIVE KRISTEN, joined the ranks of professional writers five years ago.

He had previously achieved some notoriety as the creator of the popular folk song THE PHANTOM FLASHER. His ambition is to write the kind of filmscripts that force him to work with beautiful women in exotic locations.

Clive is a contributor to a number of national publications which include LE MAGAZINE and FOOTBALL MONTHLY. He is best known in the regionally as an occasional feature writer for the YORKSHIRE POST.

The Ghost Trails series began with the popular GHOST TRAILS OF NORTHUMBRIA. Further companion volumes to this title - MORE GHOST TRAILS OF NORTHUMBRIA, and MURDER AND MYSTERY TRAILS OF NORTHUMBRIA were inflicted on the world in 1993. The author has also recently completed ' HOW TO BUY AND RENT PROPERTY IN FRANCE - a specialist guide, offering independent advice to those considering the advantages of property on the warmer side of the channel. A first novel, FROST AND FIRE, is in preparation, and Clive is soon to co-write an account of the Falklands War.

The Illustrator

The cover and map designs again show two creative facets in the wide repertoire of MARK NUTTALL's skills as an illustrator. His cover for the first GHOST TRAILS book was considered to be an important reason for the impact of the book. Naturally he was invited to illustrate the next two volumes in the NORTHUMBRIA TRAILS HERITAGE SERIES.

Together with the author Mark created RAMBO THE GIANT FERRET. First featured in newsprint on April 1st. 1989, RAMBO has passed into local folklore as the scourge of a Northumbrian valley.

Mark's relationship with the author began with an unfortunate encounter a Lancashire classroom. The author was the English teacher : the illustrator the pupil. Despite this handicap Mark is now semi-literate. His respect for the author is indicated by the fact that he keeps a picture of him mounted below the cistern of the smallest room in his cottage.

Mark, who is currently working in graphic design for television, is also noted for his distinctive cartoon strips. He is presently illustrating a cartoon book - THE AMAZON WOMAN - inspired by his life's partner, the ever-forgiving Helen.

Tynan Weir.
June 1994

Ghost Trails of the Yorkshire Dales

Contents

Trail One -   Wharfedale, Wensleydale
and Coverdale.   Page 1

Trail Two -   Bolton, Blubberhouses
and Grassington.   Page 41

Trail Three -   Nidderdale, Ripon and
Fountains Abbey.   Page 81

Trail Four -   Gargrave, Skipton and
Wharfedale.   Page 107

Trail Five -   Kirkby Stephen, Swaledale
and Tan Hill.   Page 139

Trail Six -   Dent, Lunesdale, and
Ribblesdale.   Page 159

Historical Notes/Glossary   Page 205

Taking Care in the Countryside

Most of the sites in this book can be accessed from public rights of way. Where this does not happen visitors can get a good impression of a site from suggested viewpoints.

Much of the land is farmed, and should be treated with respect. In a few cases, access is restricted and the necessary consents should be obtained. Special care is required during the lambing season and visitors are requested to follow the guidelines of the country code. Please follow footpaths, close gates, and keep dogs under close control. Litter is unsightly and can cause injury and suffering to animals.

Some of the buildings mentioned are private homes. Please do not trespass or behave intrusively. Property owners have been generous in the information they have provided. Please ensure their quiet and privacy is preserved.

These tours are designed for the motorist and none of the walks suggested are arduous. Nevertheless, Dales weather can be unpredictable - even in summer. It is suggested that visitors do not walk alone. They should have adequate footwear and a waterproof garment. A good map and compass are also highly recommended.

The Author

The National Park

Large sections of these trails fall within the Yorkshire Dales National Park. It is an area of almost 700 square miles that contains some of the most delightful fells and moorland in Great Britain.

The Yorkshire Dales National Park has enjoyed considerable success in balancing the disparate needs of visitors and those who live and work within its boundaries. There are many examples of the way in which the National Park has brought people together. One important example is conservation - a continuous process in which considerable success has been achieved through the work of volunteers under the guidance of the Park's experts.

The National Park itself has been a major catalyst in changing the public perception and awareness of this splendidly untamed corner of England. There is something here for everyone, but the emphasis is on quiet enjoyment and personal responsibility. The National Park itself provides car parks, picnic areas, excellent information centres, and even one of the best cafes in the UK. But most of all, the National Park has created a comprehensive framework of access, through waymarking and the maintainence of paths and bridleways.

The Yorkshire Dales National Park deserves our support, not least because it is a good idea that actually works. Please bear this in mind as you enjoy the unique magic of the area. Happy Trails.

Clive Kristen and Mark Nuttall. Fans of the National Park.

Ghost Trails of the Yorkshire Dales

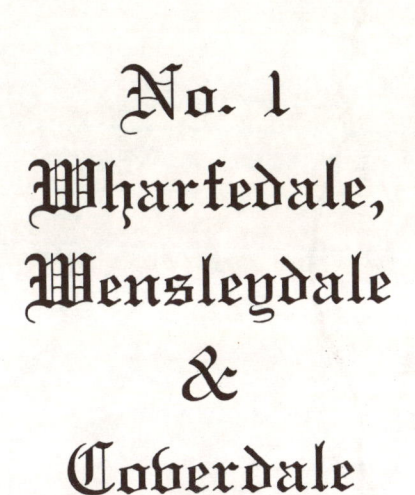

No. 1
Wharfedale, Wensleydale & Coverdale

This circular motoring tour takes approximately ten hours

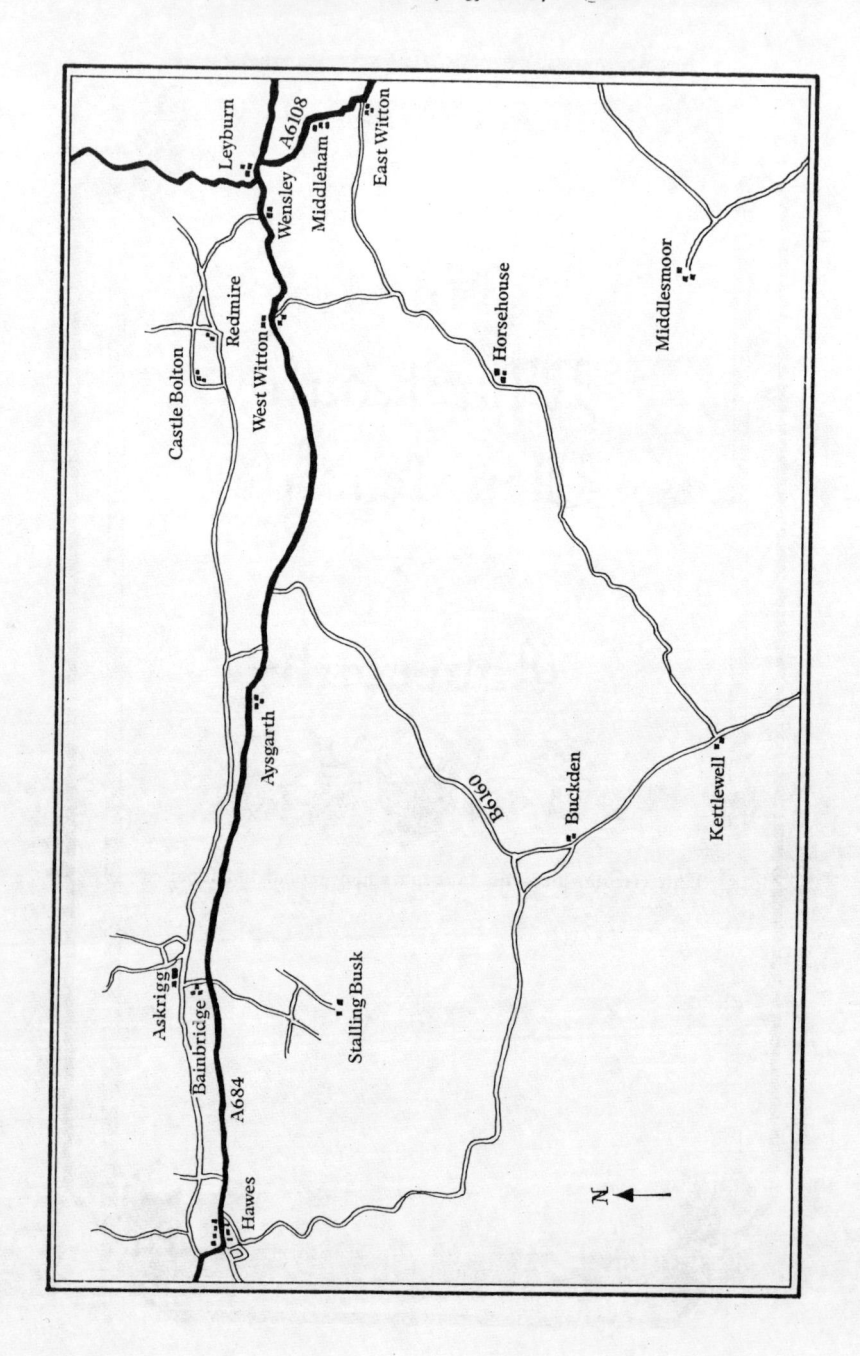

Ghost Trails of the Yorkshire Dales

Making A Fast Buck

Buckden is a delightful place to begin the serious business of ghosthunting.

A stone cross a mile from the village marks the limit of the ancient Forest of Langstroth - a Norman Deer preserve. Throughout the Middle Ages poaching was a problem for the landowner. Particularly when times were tough there were always those courageous enough to risk everything for the chance of a venison roast.

Those caught rarely enjoyed the privilege of a trial. The lucky poacher would be tied to a tree for a whipping that stripped the flesh from his spine. The less fortunate would suffer the savage cut of the woodsman's axe as it removed his hand or foot. Habitual poachers were hung from a convenient tree and the body was left to putrefy. This edifying spectacle was said to have a deterrent effect on those who sought to steal the fruits of the forest.

The Frantic Fiddlers

Buckden has a long tradition of music and folk dancing. In the past the famous 'frantic fiddlers' were self-taught, and some of the popular playing styles have been copied and developed by the latest generation of musicians.

The Fleece Market

The visitor's focus of attention is the famous Georgian Buck Inn. This is one of the classic inns of the Dales with a deserved reputation for good food and drink. The delightful restaurant was once the local fleece market.

The Ghost Of A Thirsty Man

There is an odd apparition associated with the inn. The figure of a tall man lurching towards the main doorway was witnessed many times during the long hot summer of 1879. The man wore a collarless grubby white shirt with rolled sleeves, baggy trousers and braces, and heavy working boots. He was always in the kind of hurry that suggested a mission of great importance. But, just as he reached the open doorway, the phantom began to fade.

It is whispered that the (now redundant) ghost was that of the blacksmith, whose habit it was to rush to the inn at the end of each working session. He would order half a gallon of ale and pour it down his throat as quickly as possible. Then he would wipe his mouth on his sleeve, laugh heartily, and make his way home. The ritual, repeated twice daily, was said to last for less than three minutes.

Tradition has it that the blacksmith had a fatal seizure whilst working at his forge. This was therefore a thirsty ghost...

The haunting continued for several weeks until the Buck regulars decided to try an unusual form of exorcism. In a short ceremony, four pints of beer were ritually poured over the recently filled grave.

The Buck Inn, Buckden

The ghostly blacksmith was never seen again.

Turn left out of Buckden on the minor road towards Hawes. Cross the bridge to Hubberholme.

Daniel Thwaites, an accountant from Leeds, recalls an incident that occurred here one afternoon in July 1991.

The Phantom Picnic

" My wife Emily and I have often enjoyed a picnic down by the bridge. We carried sandwiches and wine, but couldn't get to our usual spot because another family had beaten us to it. I remember feeling annoyed at the time.

" There were four of them. The parents were around our own age - mid 30's - and the youngsters were around ten years old. They were very attractive girls. I'm pretty sure they were twins.

" What was odd about the family was their clothing. It was very 'Upstairs' Edwardian. But at the time it didn't really seem that strange. You accept what you see. We thought maybe it was some kind of fancy dress occasion.

" When they'd finished eating, the two girls went to play amongst the rocks by the riverside. We almost forgot about them until we heard the scream. It was like icy fingers on your spine. It echoed for a long time.

" We saw what had happened immediately. One of the girls had fallen on the rocks and she was lying in a heap. She was very still. It was the other girl who'd screamed. Her father was rushing to help. I tried to get up, but it was as if there was a weight on my shoulders. Emily told me later it was like the cinema. You know you're watching something that's not real.

" The little girl was scooped up from the stones by her father. She was like a little bundle of laundry in his arms. There was no sign of injury. But she was so silent. So still.

" Her father carried her gently up to the road, and the others followed silently. Just as they passed from our sight there was another scream, as loud and chilling as the first. This broke the spell. We left our things where they were and rushed up to the bridge. But there was nothing to be seen. No car. No people. Nothing. It was a strange feeling. We both knew that we'd seen a ghostly re-enactment.

" We tried to find out something about it, but there was no record of a local incident that matched the one we'd seen. But we talked about a great deal. My sister-in-law found the answer a few months later at a library in Darlington.

" What she came across was a newspaper report from 1906. The paper carried a brief account of a holiday accident that had afflicted a well-to-do family from Middleton St. George in Teesdale. It seems that one of the family's twin daughters had fallen as she played by the river at Hubberholme. There was no account of the injuries, but the accident had obviously proved fatal because the article ended by detailing the arrangements for the funeral."

Tups and Yewes, Hubberholme

Follow the high moorland road towards Hawes

A Deadly Duel

A celebrated 16th. century fight took place at Outershaw - close to where the Bunkhouse stands today. The story is that a local farmer's wife enjoyed a more than friendly liaison with her husband's brother for several years. Eventually misguided gossip alerted the husband's suspicions and he laid his trap to catch them.

The farmer, Matthew Grigghall, told his wife that he was to rise early to seek out the best of the bargains at Hawes Market. He saddled his pony, but left the animal tethered a mile away. Then he returned to the farm.

A ripple of laughter flowed from his bedroom, and when he pushed the door open his suspicions were confirmed.

The brothers agreed to settle the matter with a duel. Matthew, as the cuckolded husband, was offered the choice of weapons. He selected pitchforks. The fight took place in an open field at noon the following day. Some say Matthew improved his chances by sharpening the fork points and treating them with poison.

Neither man gave any quarter in the fight. But it was Matthew who suffered the serious wound when his brother, Mark, thrust the fork deep into his ribs. He was helped to his bed by his brother, and the now repentant wife, Rachel.

His life hung in the balance for several days, but a combination of warm ale and hot poultices did the trick. As soon as Matthew was fit enough to return to work, Mark announced his intention to leave the farm. He never returned.

Seven months later Rachel gave birth to a son, and it is said the family were happy enough for several years. But Rachel had a secret that reminded her of her lost lover. When Matthew fell seriously ill she confided the secret to him, but refused to let him disinherit her son. Some say that Rachel smothered her dying husband.

Making A Spectre Of Himself

Who can say if the Outershaw ghost was the spirit of that same Matthew Grigghall?

Certainly the phantom was seen regularly for more than a century after the death of the farmer. Dales diarist, the Reverend William Pierce, wrote in 1671 :

' The Outershaw Spectre is a most singular phenomenon. He manifests (himself) as a man who sits at the wayside trenchantly anguished. He who passes by may see (him) and hear too such wails of discomfiture (that he) makes. Upon approaching (him) the poor spectre will evanesce, leaving only a pool of tears upon the earth.

'I have not seen (him) myself. Yet from reputation few demur. This is no demon, but (the) phantasm of a tormented soul.'

Gayle Force

Continue to the summit of the moor, before enjoying the classic descent to Hawes through Gayle.

Glorious Gayle

The stark bleakness of the upper moor is the harsher face of the Dales countryside. Emily Bronte would have loved it, as do most of the residents. They are well-equipped for the climate - with woollen coats and four legs.

The view from above Gayle is breathtaking, and the village itself is one of the gems of the Dales. The weir near the heart of the village is a crashing cascade of water.

The Head Of Wensleydale

Hawes has much to recommend it. For a start there is a large car park by the Tourist Information Centre which is run by the National Park. It offers lively displays, a traditional Yorkshire Dales welcome, and a deep mine of information to all visitors.

A visit to the traditional ropemakers is highly recommended. In addition to seeing this ancient craft come alive, the delightful shop is an Aladdin's Cave of possibilities for the macrame buff. A visit to Elijah Allen's cheeseshop is a kind of pilgrimage for those who enjoy the very best examples of the cheesemaker's art.

Cheese Wars

Cheese has been important to Hawes for a long time. The Wensleydale Cheese Factory was founded in 1897. In 1935 there was a famous battle against closure. The main protagonists were the legendary Kit Lambert and the Milk Marketing Board.

Kit managed to out-manoeuvre the board with almost every throw of the dice. At the same time he tried to persuade local farmers that their own interest lay in protecting this outlet for their milk. Finally he raised the money for a cooperative buy-out of the factory. But it was a close-run thing. Victory depended on last-minute support and every penny raised.

A similar battle was fought in the early 1990's. Again the factory survived, largely through the efforts of a local publicity machine that mustered support from some rather unlikely sources. Happily Wensleydale cheese remains alive and well in Wensleydale, and the local variety is still the very best you can get.

A Sobering Thought

The Temperance movement was very strong around Hawes, and it is still possible to enjoy a relaxing hour at the inn where no alcohol is served.

There was strong rivalry between those who enjoyed a tipple, and those who had signed the pledge. On one occasion a vociferous group of temperance women blockaded a local hostelry because the licensee had publicly insulted one of their number. Tempers flared and handbags were swung in anger. A middle-aged farmer collapsed to his knees and had to be carried home. He died some six weeks later.

An Inebriate Spirit

It is said that a red-nosed ghost, with bottle in hand, mingles with the crowd on market days. One famous appearance was at the opening of a Hawes Summer Gala in the late 1970's. A well known face from the little mourned TV Soap 'Crossroads' had been booked for the official opening. The actor was steadily performing (with more ham than Sainsbury's) when a red-nosed character in the crowd shouted ' sirreverence.'

The actor paused for a moment, and his eyes picked out the heckler.

" What did you say? " he enquired.

" Sirreverence, " came the reply.

" But I'm no reverence, " said the soap star, " merely a humble actor."

One or two people in the crowd began to giggle, and the actor looked decidedly nervous. He cut what was left of his speech, and announced the Gala open. There was muted applause as the actor stepped down from his podium.

Then an odd thing happened. A noise described as 'something between laughter and lightning' echoed from the PA. The actor was alarmed. He climbed up to his perch again, tapped the microphone, and shrugged his shoulders.

" I don't know what that was, " he said. Then he thought of a joke. He looked heavenwards and said : " But if I was a reverence, perhaps I'd be able to tell you? "

As he made this comment he looked down towards the heckler. Other eyes followed his. The little red-nosed man had vanished. Where he had been standing there was a clear empty space in the crowd.

For moment time seemed to stand still. People looked at the empty space, then back to the actor.

" Well I won't be able to get his autograph now, will I? " he joked.

This comment diffused the situation. Soon it would be forgotten, except perhaps by those who had been standing close to the heckler.

Tony Clarke, a Gala visitor from Bradford recalls : " It was the the weirdest thing. We were hemmed in pretty tightly but he was there one moment and gone the next. But there's no way he could have moved away without us noticing. Even after he'd gone there was a strange smell. My girlfriend reckoned it was whisky on the breath, but I'm not sure. It was sweeter and stronger than that - a bit like silage. "

'Sirreverence' also takes some explaining. As a dialect word it had almost died out by the late 1970's. Today it is not heard at all.

One school of thought is that it was a corruption of the phrase 'Save your reverence', but there is a more likely derivation.

In the Comedy of Errors Shakespeare has Dromio speaking of an malodorous woman : " Such a one as a man may not speak of without he say 'sirreverence'."

The meaning in Romeo and Juliet is perhaps more clear. Mercutio says : " We'll draw thee from the mire of this sir-reverence love, wherein thou stick't up to the ears."

If there are lingering doubts, there is full clarification in Richard Head's 'English Rogue' (1665). In this bawdy classic he has a man 'sirreverencing in paper and running to the window with it.'

It seems that the red-nosed ghost of Hawes was passing a comment, not a compliment, to the former star of Crossroads...

Take the A684 towards Leyburn, and divert via Burtersett to Semerwater.

Semerwater is a lovely little lake, and an oasis of tranquillity.

Sunset above Semerwater

The Drowned City

There is not a shred of physical evidence, but the tradition remains that beneath the waters you will find the ruins of a lost city.

It is said that a beggar once called at the city asking for shelter, but the only people who would take him in were an old couple who lived on the hillside. The next morning the beggar vanished and the flooding began. Three days later the roof tops disappeared beneath the water.

Continue along the A684 to Askrigg

TV Times

Askrigg is not Herriot's 'Darrowby'. The BBC's selected Askrigg for the All Creatures Great and Small series, because Thirsk (the original focus of the books) had changed beyond all recognition.

James Herriot's Darrowby

One of the powers of television is to create popular mythology. By seeking a village that captured the very essence of life in the 1940's and 50's, they turned back the clock. To millions of viewers Askrigg will always be 'Darrowby'. An imposing early 19th. c. house opposite the church remains recognisably 'Skeldale House'. The Kings Arms is the 'Drovers Arms'.

Romeo And Juliet?

Mill Gill, located at the side of the church, leads upwards for a mile to a ravine. This will for ever be associated with a bloodthirsty killing that took place early in the 16th. c.

Two bodies were found at the narrowest point of the ravine. One was a young man, the other little more than a girl. Their hair had been hacked away and knotted into bonds that tied the wrists. The cause of death was not immediately clear, but the surgeon's investigation concluded that a narrow blade or pin had been inserted through an ear into the brain.

From their clothes it was clear that both young people were gipsies. It was believed that the killing was probably the 'revenge' of a local farmer who believed that the problems he had suffered with curdled milk were the product of a gipsy curse. No charges were brought and the case has never been explained.

But a more modern theory suggests that the killings were linked to an inter-family or 'clan' feud. There is contemporary evidence of rivalry between gipsy families in this corner of England. It could easily be that the young victims of this dreadful crime were subject to a Romeo and Juliet style blood feud. This kind of killing is associated with sacrifice and ritualistic cleansing. The cutting of hair is said to indicate the submission of the victim.

A Good Nap

Mary Queen of Scots stayed for two nights at Nappa Hall whilst technically a prisoner at Bolton Castle. It is said that this brief relaxation of her regime was beneficial, and that she slept particularly well. Nappa Hall is now a farm.

A Haunted Hide And Seek

In 1878 there was another guest at the farm. This young visitor played hide and seek with her friend in the long hall. The room was lit only by firelight and a few candles.

A figure approached from the darkened end of the room. This was a woman dressed in a Tudor style black velvet dress. The young girl reached out towards her. The woman turned and smiled before moving off towards the stairs.

The child talked later about what she had seen. She recognised Queen Mary from a miniature portrait. The stairs from the hall lead towards the turret room in which the Queen had spent her nights at the hall.

The ghost of Mary Queen of Scots is one of the best-travelled in the UK. There have been claimed sightings at nearby Bolton Castle, at the Old Manor Castle in Sheffield, and at Holyrood and Fotheringay. But the most celebrated sighting was in 1908 at Temple Newsham House in Leeds. Here the ghost was seen by Lord Halifax.

This last sighting is particularly odd. The rest of Mary's haunts are all associated with episodes in her tragic life. There is no evidence that Mary ever stayed in Leeds, but the house is said to be the birthplace of Lord Darnley. He was Mary's (murdered) second husband. Could this be a case of one ghost visiting the old haunts of another?

Poet's Dotty Honeymoon

In 1802 Wordsworth and his young wife enjoyed part of their honeymoon at Aysgarth. The signs that love would not always run smoothly were already evident. The Lakeland Bard had insisted on inviting the 'sister of my soul' to accompany them. Dorothy Wordsworth, and William's young bride - Mary - were as much in tune as a junior school band. But the unlikely threesome put a brave face on things for their Dales tour. They also visited Bolton and Middleham Castles.

A young vet, later to become famous as James Herriot, spent a more conventional honeymoon night in a local hostelry. The name, in the hotel register, will be pointed out to customers who ask nicely...

Continue along A684 to Aysgarth

A Phantom Coach?

There are recurring tales of a phantom coach and four that is said to be seen around Aysgarth, and at locations in the upper valley. But the stories are so varied in the telling that it seems to make a credible haunting unlikely.

A Famous Falls

The Aysgarth Falls have attracted a rich array of artists, poets, writers, and film makers.

Middle Falls are as spectacular as anything you will see in the Dales. Robin Hood fought Little John here for a Warner Brothers blockbuster in 1990.

Not at swashbuckling as Kevin Costner perhaps, but the artist JMW Turner did brave the deepest of puddles for the chance to sketch Middle Falls and Yore Mill Bridge after heavy rain. On a more tranquil day he completed a famous painting of the Lower Falls.

The Spectral Shuffle

Follow the woodland path from the National park Centre. The Upper Falls can been seen from the bridge, as can Yore Mill.

This famous mill began life in 1784. It was first used for corn, then flax, and finally wool. The building now houses the Yorkshire Carriage Museum - possibly the best collection of vehicles in the UK. Here you will find everything from dog carts to fire engines.

There is even a haunted cab, but this is one story best left to the enthusiastic telling of the museum staff.

Tradition has it that the mill has another restless spirit. This is the ghost of the son of a former mill owner who became over-familiar with several of the younger female handloom weavers. It is said that they extracted a terrible revenge for his unwanted attentions.

This phantom emits wails which are pitched above the normal register, and his ghostly walk is said to more of a spectral shuffle.

Traditional Yorkshire Fare

The Yore Mill Gift Shop is also worth a visit, and the Mill Race Tea Shop offers some of the very best traditional Yorkshire cooking. One belt-busting speciality is rich fruit cake served with Wensleydale cheese.

Continue for one mile along the A684, before diverting for Bolton Castle via Carperby

The Knight's Tale

Castle Bolton stands on the northern slopes of Wensleydale, once known as Yoredale. The task of fortifying the manor house of Richard, Lord Scrope, began in 1379

As Lord Chancellor of England to King Richard II, Richard Scrope was a man of massive influence. He also encouraged the flowering talent of a former diplomat, Geoffrey Chaucer. The poet responded by using Richard Scrope as the model for his Knight's Tale. This was a great compliment as 'The knight' embodied all the finer points of chivalry - which was perhaps a fair reflection of the model. Consequently the story is one of the longest, and most tedious, of the Canterbury Tales.

Without Planning Permission

Richard Scrope contracted mason John Lewyn to build 'a tower for a kitchen, and a gatehouse and other buildings to be vaulted and embattled.' But there was a little unchivalrous cheating here. Lord Scrope had permission to build towers 50 feet in height and other buildings to '40 feet below the battlements.' The finished towers were rather more than 100 feet, and the whole building was much better fortified than the 'planning permission' permitted. Nevertheless Richard got away with it. He could have argued that the building was still rather more residential than military, and that the position - with higher ground to the north - was less than strategically ideal. Nevertheless it was very solidly built. Local tradition has it that the mortar was mixed with fresh ox blood.

Mary Queen Of Scots

The so-called 'Mary's Room' is perhaps an unlikely apartment for the captive Queen. The state apartments were in the north-west tower.

Queen Mary was held in 'honourable custody' after suffering defeat at the Battle of Lanside in 1568. The choice of Bolton Castle for six months of her incarceration is an unusual one. The greatest division between the Scots and English crowns was religion. The choice of the Catholic Scope family has been said to reflect just how much they were trusted as loyal subjects of Queen Elizabeth.

Queen Mary's retinue included 40 men to look after 20 carriage and 23 saddle horses. The Queen also enjoyed the services of six personal attendants.

It is clear that Lady Scrope had not expected quite so many guests. She had to borrow beds and other furniture from her friends.

Mary spent much of her imprisonment in a room in the south-west tower. Her obvious boredom was reflected by the studious way she used a diamond ring to carve her name - 'Marie R' - on one of the windows. The window survived the attacks of the Civil War, but not the clumsiness of a workman instructed to remove the glass to take it for safe-keeping at Bolton Hall.

The Queen of Scots was not always confined to the castle. Her visit to Nappa Hall has been mentioned, and a number of other social visits were allowed. She also rode with the local hunt.

The Catholic Queen of Scots was a political hot potato. This explains why she was held in nine different castles during 18 years of imprisonment. Of these, only Bolton Castle survives to this day.

Mary was eventually brought to trial for her 'crimes.' She denied to the end any part in plotting against Queen Elizabeth. But this denial is as questionable as a party political broadcast. The Queen of Scots attracted fierce loyalties, and despite the close attention of Queen Elizabeth's spies, always managed to stay in touch with the game.

She was executed on 8th. February 1587 at Fotheringay.

The Not-so-great Escape

The Queen made one famous escape bid from Bolton Castle. She climbed out of the window and managed to dodge the guards. She hid for a while to make sure her escape was undetected, then took the path down towards the Leyburn road. Once she was sure of her bearings she moved swiftly along the hill side.

She almost made it to Leyburn. But when she heard the pursuit, she panicked. As she ran her shawl became entangled in a briar, and she did not stop to retrieve it. This was a fatal mistake. Her pursuers found the shawl, which convinced them they were on the right track. The queen was captured a few minutes later.

The area of hillside where these events took place is still known as Leyburn Shawl. It is not certain however that this is connected to the escape. The old norse word 'schalle' means a shelter, and there is good evidence of a pre-historic settlement below. To confuse matters further, the Saxon word 'shaw' means wood. This leaves us with three possibilities for 'Leyburn Shawl'. The escape story is perhaps the least likely, but most alluring. It is certainly a striking coincidence.

A Fine Year's Work

Bolton Castle was besieged in 1644 and held out for more than a year against the Roundheads. John Scrope, who held it for the king, was fined 7000 for his efforts. He died in London two years later at the age of 20.

In 1647 the Commonwealth Committee order that the castle be 'rendered untenable.'

No Smoke Without Fire

The floor area of the dungeon was just 53 square feet. The unfortunate prisoners were dropped through a square trap door to the stone floor eight feet below. There was a fixed iron staple to which more troublesome prisoners could be chained.

The dungeon also contained special hooded chimneys. The hoods were placed over a central hearth, and smoke was dispersed through a series of pipes. Such comfort was ridiculed by the guards. It is known that from time to time they would block the pipes with wet rags to ensure that the prisoners suffered for the warmth of their fire.

The Kilted Ghost

One of the castle's ghosts is said to be that of prisoner from a later conflict.

An unnamed Scotsman captured after the Battle of Preston(1715) was thrown into the dungeon or oubliette. The fall broke his neck.

There have been glimpses of an unusual spectre over the years. A kilted figure is said to rise above the position of the trap door and hover alarmingly in mid air. The draught from below ruffles the pleats of his kilt.

The face is said to be knotted in pain, with the jaw and neck set at unnatural angles. There is a ashen pallor to the face, which makes the blood-red lips, and the low groan that passes between them, even more alarming.

This grisly spectre is said to rotate slowly, as if taking in the full 360 degree panorama. But once the full turn is complete the vision fades rapidly away. Witnesses have said all that remains is a chill in the air and the faint aroma of smoked fish.

A Sorry Selection Of Spooks

The most celebrated ghost at Bolton Castle is said to be that of Mary Queen of Scots.

Unhappily there are no records of sightings in recent years, which has lead to suggestions that the Queen is now a redundant wraith.

The shades of many former prisoners were also said to put in regular appearances until the final years of the 19th. century. Again there is little evidence to suggest continuing manifestation, but there are enough groans and sighs heard on the breeze to encourage the determined ghost trailer.

Return to the A684 and follow the road to West Witton

The famous tradition of West Witton is linked to ancient beliefs.

The Burning Of Bartle

On the Saturday closest to August 24th. each year (St. Bartholomew's Day) a straw effigy is carried through the village before being burnt on a bonfire.

Bartholomew is perhaps the unlikeliest of saints. In the synoptic gospels he is mentioned only by name in the list of apostles. Though very little is known about him, this has not prevented any number of traditions becoming associated with his name.

The Syrian tradition is that his original name was Jesus, but stronger orthodoxy suggest the name is a patronymic for Nathaniel Bartolmai.

According to Eusebius he embarked on a missionary tour of India after the Ascension. The horror of his martyrdom is certainly the reason for his popularity. It is said that Bartholomew was flayed alive and then crucified with his head downwards. In works of art he is generally represented with a large knife - the instrument of his martyrdom - or (as in Michaelangelo's 'Last Judgement') with his skin hanging over his arm.

It is difficult to imagine a link between this and the chant used each time the Bartle effigy comes to rest during the tour of West Witton .

At Pen Hill Crags he tore his rags
At Hunter's Thorn he blew his horn
At Capleback he brake his knee
At Grassgill Beck he brake his neck
At Wadham's End he couldn't fend
At Grassgill End he made his end. Shout lads, shout.

The rhyme is said to be a loose interpretation of the story of an 18th. century swine thief who was hunted on the fells, captured, and hung.

There is a strange mixture here of both local and Christian tradition. The effigy and bonfire though may have rather more to do with paganism. It is the same contradiction of cultural roots which gives us holly, ivy and yule logs at Christmas, and the egg (as a symbol of fertility and regeneration) at Easter.

Follow the A684 into Leyburn

Leyburn is frequently overlooked by visitors. It is not perhaps the most attractive of Dales towns, but it is certainly one of the most welcoming. Leyburn is also an excellent touring base for exploring some of the most dramatic and unspoilt corners of the Yorkshire Dales.

The Sound Of The Horn

The splendid Posthorn Cafe is associated with Wensleydale's most elusive manifestation - the phantom coach and horses.

The Age Of The Resurrectionists

A former landlord of the Black Swan Inn was suspected of being involved with the resurrectionists.

During the early years of the 19th. century the demand for cadavers for dissection by medical students, reached its zenith. As the value of a corpse declined rapidly with decomposition, fresh graves were closely guarded. But the trade was so valuable there were always those prepared to take risks.

The most famous exponents were Burke and Hare, who supplied bodies to anatomists in Edinburgh. They supplemented 'churchyard stock' with their own murder victims. After turning King's Evidence, William Hare admitted he had 'combined with William Burke to cause the death of 15 persons.' The real number is unknown, but 50 is likely to be nearer the mark.

In Leyburn the problem was never so serious, but a number of graves were robbed. The best market for fresh cadavers could be as far away as Durham and York. This meant that it sometimes took several days to negotiate the terms of sale and delivery. In this unpredictable business it was rare to have orders placed in advance.

A cold store was required for the corpses, and it is said that the cellars of the Black Swan proved to be ideal.

The authorities had their suspicions. The building was raided on several occasions, but nothing beyond jewellery (inconclusively linked to the missing occupant of a disturbed grave) was found. Nobody was charged with a crime.

Public concern put considerable pressure on those who required bodies for dissection. The market declined steeply. By the middle of the 19th. century this grisly trade had all but disappeared.

Take the road signposted 'Ripon'. Cross the River Ure before Middleham and cross the turreted iron girder bridge. Then turn left again towards Middleham.

A Place In History

The building of Middleham Castle began during the last quarter of the 13th. century. The keep, which dates almost completely from this period, is one of the largest in England.

The castle was said to be the favourite residence of Richard III - the most maligned monarch in English history. His son, Edward, was born here.

Much of what can be seen today are the additions of the 14th. and 15th. centuries. The castle is greatly ruined but is nevertheless well worth a visit.

Durant's Delicacies

The delightful village also has much to offer the visitor. Durant's Tea Shop is recommended for a pit stop. The menu includes the best game pies in the north and the excellent Yorkshire Curd Tarts.

Treasure Hunters

The area close to the castle's former hunting lodge has become popular with treasure hunters.

The number of swords and rings found at the site encouraged a small army of metal-detectives.

Perhaps the most important find was the gold and enamel Middleham Jewel that was purchased for £2.5 million by the Yorkshire Museum.

But the most interesting find was made by a Darlington decorator in 1993. Mr. William Caygill unearthed three earthenware jugs which contained more than 5000 coins. It is the largest single find from the English Civil War period.

The French Princess Henrietta Maria - the young consort of King Charles I - visited Amsterdam in 1643. Her mission was to raise as much money as possible for the royalist cause. She took with her valuables that included part of the Crown Jewels.

The Middleton find is said to represent part of the cash she brought back to England. Why these coins came to be buried in the Middleton mud is less certain. One possibility is a military threat to the castle but historians have argued this is unlikely. The answer is probably more mundane. The English banking system had collapsed so rather more old fashioned ways of depositing large sums of money had become necessary. It is likely that those entrusted with hiding the money also became victims of the war.

Take the A6108 to Jervaulx. The car park is on the right by the green bungalow. £1 fee - honesty box

A Splendid Ruin

Jervaulx is more heavily mutilated than the other major Yorkshire abbeys, but as a ruin it has a particular fascination. During the 19th. century ivy took a hold on much of the ancient masonry. It added to the attraction but accelerated the decay.

In its heyday Jervaulx was famous for cheese. The monks were also noted for the training of horses - an art still practised by nationally renowned training stables in the area.

The name derives from the River Ure (formerly Yore). This spot has also been referred to in history as Yorevale, Jervaulx and Jarvis. It was the Marchioness of Ailesbury who adopted the French spelling.

The French connection began with a Normandy monk called Peter de Quincy. His determination to found a religious house in Yorkshire was based on the rumour that the population were in particularly dire need of the civilizing influence of Christianity.

Peter de Quincy belonged to an offshoot branch of the Order of St. Benedict. By 1149 this Order of Savigny merged with their Cistercian landlords. The unfortunately named Akar Fitzbardolph made a grant of land to the monks, and his brother (Alan, Earl of Richmond) gave the monks pasturage.

The first small establishment was at Fors (1158), but the poor land did not provide a living. The story is that a vision of the Virgin and Child guided the unhappy monks through dense woodland until they arrived at the present site on the banks of the Ure.

Certainly the new site was better for business. At its most prosperous the abbey owned half the Ure valley. The effigy of Henry Fitzhugh, a descendant of the Earl of Richmond, can be found at the centre of the ruined church. This greatest of the abbey's benefactors died in 1307.

The effigy is well worn, but is recognisable as a knight in armour. It is a fine example of the carving skills associated with Durham sculptors.

The abbey prospered until the 16th. century when there were clear signs of corruption. It was dissolved by Henry VIII. The last abbot, Adam of Sedbergh, sold the abbey plate to help finance the Pilgrimage of Grace.

Adam was convicted of treason and executed at the Tower of London. As he waited for his trail he carved his name in his cell. It is still visible today.

The present ruinous state is a sad tribute to the enthusiasm of Thomas Cromwell's demolition crew.

A Celebrated Spectre

The ghost of Adam of Sedbergh has been quiet in recent years. This contrasts with the fanfare of stomach curdling wails that used to announce the appearances of this troubled spirit.

This was, by all accounts, a premier league haunting. The grizzled head was carried neatly beneath the arm with the jagged work of the axeman clearly displayed around the neck. The executioner was apparently a trainee who took seven blows to accomplish what should have been achieved in two or three at the most. The abbot's attendants, and even battle hardened soldiers, fainted during the proceedings.

The face of the ghost was acclaimed by Victorian ghosthunter, Henry Muir, as the 'most hideous and pitiful spectacle.' Muir's account concludes :

'The eyes roll upwards in their sockets, and the lines above are chiselled as though by a mason. The blackened tongue moves most copiously without its orifice, shaping words interpreted by witnesses variously. But the sound presaging this exhibition is a cry more mournful than that of the huntsman's dog. Take good counsel and turn from the sound, for the visitation is more dreadful than any I have known.'

It should be noted that Muir often worked for patrons who knew he value of advertising. Indeed rather too many of his 'visitations' fall into the 'most hideous and pitiful' category. Nevertheless the account is chilling, even by Muir standards, and visitors of a nervous disposition are given the appropriate health warning.

Return towards Middleham, turning left by the village green at East Witton.

East Witton is a delightful village set around a large village green. It is also the setting for a classic ghost story.

The Big Man Of Braithwaite

The Big Man of Braithwaite is never referred to by name, but is understood to be a licentious former Lord of the Manor.

It seems that the Big Man took a fancy to a village girl called Annie. He tried all the usual tricks to overcome her resistance, but Annie was fiercely determined to preserve her virtue.

At last the Big Man agreed to marry her, but explained that for 'family reasons' their union must remain secret. The wedding would therefore be a quiet affair.

Annie suspected treachery, but was reassured when it was agreed that her sister could attend the ceremony. The service was performed expeditiously. As soon as the ceremonial was completed the Big Man called for wine and instructed that the warming pan be made ready.

The following morning Annie awoke to find her husband had gone, but the chamber door was locked. After dark he returned with food and wine and the desire for an action replay.

She fought off his advances, but was persuaded to join him beneath the sheets by the knowledge that her sister was held prisoner.

For two further days the pattern of lust and loathing was repeated. Finally Annie could stand it no more. She spent the day sharpening a quilting pin, and when she heard footsteps positioned herself behind the door.

As the shadowy figure entered the room she struck out and upwards with her pin. There was a choked cry of pain and the body slumped to the floor. Annie knew immediately that something was wrong. She knelt on the floor and the face that was caught in the moonlight was that of her dying sister. The pin was lodged deep in her throat, and blood was pumping from the severed artery.

Annie made her escape towards West Witton, but was intercepted on the road by the Big Man and members of his hunting party. She was forced to return to the hall, and the price of covering up the murder of her sister was predictable.

A month later Annie declared herself pregnant. This gave her instant respite from his attentions, but she was also relegated to the role of servant. Within a matter of days the Big Man had installed a new mistress.

The new mistress - Sarah - soon found out that life with the Big Man was less than blissful. She shared her sorrows with Annie and the two of them became partners in distress. From their discussions it became clear that both women believed themselves to be the legal wife of the Lord of the Manor. They decided to confront him together.

The Big Man laughed when they demanded the truth. He told them that both weddings had been a charade. Indeed, the part of the priest had been played by a retired gamekeeper. But they were free to go if they wished, or they could hide their shame by remaining in the house as servants.

The two women plotted their revenge. Rat poison was bought and mixed with the wine. The Big Man became ill, and for the first time in many years took to his bed alone.

They took it in turns to act as nurse. Each time they reduced the dose he felt better and his strength began to return. Each time they increased it he suffered a new bout of agony and weakness. In this manner they managed to keep him balanced between life and death for several weeks. Finally they grew impatient, and agreed the time had come to finish him off for good.

They played a game of chance for the privilege. Sarah won and administered the final massive dose of poison. Then they locked the door to the room and left him to die.

Two days later the doctor was called. The Big Man was found dead, but still warm in his bed. His longstanding illness was of course well known. Nothing was suspected.

Several months later Annie gave birth to a boy. The testimony of her friend - and a freshly forged marriage license - were enough to secure the boy's 'rights of inheritance.' Thomas was brought up at the hall by his mother and 'Aunt' Sarah. He became Lord of the Manor on his 21st. birthday.

But shortly afterwards the property was sold. Son, mother, and 'aunt' left the district immediately.

Some say this was because Thomas had set his heart on owning a plantation in the Americas. Others suggest that rekindled rumours of foul murder drove them away.

But there is another possibility. On the very eve of his inheritance Thomas had a terrible vision. It seems that a very tall man seemed to be standing at the foot of his bed. In his hand he held a goblet, which he turned upside down to show it was empty. His face was pale and his lips swollen. The deep set eyes were mirrors of pain.

Night after night the vision was repeated. Nobody knew what it meant, but Thomas became increasingly fearful, and his mother and 'aunt' increasingly upset. The only escape from the dream was to leave the house.

But perhaps, after all, they did not journey far.

For on cold winter's evenings three figures can sometimes be seen walking on the village green at West Witton. The shapes are distinctly those of a youngish man, and two women of mature years.

Some say, there is a fourth, but fainter figure behind them. It is hard to say what manner of creature this is, but in the moonlight this figure is said to cast an exceptionally long shadow.

A narrow lane leads from the Green. Pass Braithwaite Hall on the left before beginning the descent towards Coverham.

The Faintest Trace

Coverham village is built largely of stone taken from the former abbey. Another victim of the dissolution, there are a few scanty remains sited close to the river.

The abbey had previously suffered in a number of Scots raids. The White Monks who lived here were famous for their singing, and the breeding of white horses.

Steeped In History

The former Holy Trinity Church is also disused. The building stands at a strangely isolated spot outside the village. The churchyard is so steeply banked that if you stand close to the bottom of the slope it is impossible to see the church. It is also claimed it was impossible to hear the church bells, but this may have had as much to do with the rushing waters of the falls as the lie of the land. The churchyard today is a powerfully desolate place.

The Woman In Black

There is a famous walk that runs from the church to Tupgill and Fern Gill before rising gradually to Middleham Low Moor.

It is a walk that is more popular with visitors than locals. This may be because of the regular appearances - particularly around nightfall - of the famous Woman in Black.

Courting Wall Corner - once a popular meeting place for young lovers - is the most likely place to encounter this apparition. It is an unsporting venue for a haunting.

The story begins with a local lady of extraordinary beauty. She had many suitors, but finally managed to reduce her short list of marriage candidates to two.

She enjoyed the company of both men, and was clever enough to maintain both relationships without difficulty. But her family finally insisted that she make up her mind.

She agonised over her choice, and having made it decided the best way to avoid repercussions was an elopement. Unfortunately the runner-up in the marriage stakes discovered her intentions, and blackmailed her into a final assignation at Courting Wall Corner.

He pleaded with her to change her mind. But when it was clear he was the loser, he fell into a rage and strangled her. The body was buried in a shallow grave on Middleham Moor.

There were suspicions, but it proved impossible to prove anything without the corpse as evidence.

But the mysterious 'disappearance' of the young woman would not be forgotten. The regular apparition of a lady in a long black mourning coat made sure of that. These appearances took place most frequently at Courting Wall Corner and the spectre always gave good value with anguished sobs and head shaking.

Some years later peat cutters dug up a skeleton on the moor. This proved to be the remains of a young woman. Shreds of black cloth hung tenaciously to the bones.

From that time the hauntings have become less frequent. But just a few years ago a female figure in black opened a gate for some walkers before vanishing into the ether. Another group of visitors called out to her as they drove past the corner. The disappearing act once again had a predictable effect.

This Woman in Black is a spectre that is still very much on the active list.

In February 1993 a cyclist from Middleham was approaching the corner when he saw the mournful figure in the black cloak. He cycled past her and stopped. It took no more than a few seconds to turn around. He was very surprised to find she had vanished.

Later he discussed what he had seen at local hostelry. The landlord held back until the cyclist finished his meal. But when the story was told the young man became visibly distressed. It is said that the cyclist required the fortification of spirits of distilled kind that evening.

Trees near Courting Wall Corner

Recross the humpback bridge over the River Cover. Take the road signposted West Scrafton. Following this lovely section of the Cover Valley you by-pass the hamlet of Caldbergh.

Miles Of Poetry

Caldbergh's most famous son, Miles Coverdale, was born at a nearby hall in 1488. The building is now a farmhouse.

Miles was best known in his day as an orator, but is now remembered for the first complete translation of the bible in English. This landmark book (published in 1535) has not been noted as a work of great scholarship, but the poetry and beauty of the language made it a considerable literary achievement. Some of the phraseology was retained for the King James (Authorised) Bible of 1611, although the translators ultimately relied more heavily on Tyndale.

Miles Coverdale, also noted for a translation of the Apocrypha, rose from humble Yorkshire origins to become a major force in the kingdom. As Chaplain to King Edward VI he was a strong influence for reform during the king's short reign. He later became Bishop of Exeter but fell from grace on the accession of Queen Mary. He left for Denmark with two servants in 1555, but returned four years later. He preached throughout London - most notably at St. Pauls - until his death in 1568.

A Phantom Hiker?

A mile beyond Caldbergh there is a footpath that leads down to St. Simon's Bridge. Some 30 years ago there were reports of a phantom walker who stopped to ask the way before vanishing. The distinctive features of the apparition included a beard, an old-fashioned 'hacking jacket', and leather leggings. A Germanic, or possibly Scandinavian accent was also mentioned.

This kind of story is common enough in the Yorkshire Dales. If every account was believed there would hardly be a path that did not feature a phantom hiker. Most frequently these encounters take place on upper moorland tracks on misty days...

The road passes through West Scrafton. Turn left at the signpost that indicates 'Kettlewell 9 Miles.'

A Change Of Horses

There are outstanding views of classic Dales scenery from the road that now rises gently up the Cover Valley. This is truly one of the least known, but loveliest corners of England.

Horsehouse is little more than hamlet today, but it has many important historical associations.

The village is positioned on strategic routes that link Lancaster, Skipton and Middleham castles. It was also on the famous coaching route from Ripon to London, and as the name implies this was an important staging post for travellers.

A Famous Fisherman

A more modern claim to fame is that Horsehouse was chosen as the favoured country 'haunt' of Jack Charlton. As a footballer this great Geordie character won a World Cup winners medal with England, and helped Leeds United to a bag full of silverware. Later he proved his worth as a manager with Middlesbrough before taking the Republic of Ireland to two World Cup finals. Given the meagre resources he was able to muster for both jobs it could easily be argued that Jack Charlton ranks alongside the greatest football managers of all time.

A Noted Hostelry

The late 17th. century Thwaite Arms is justly famous for fine ales and good bar food. It is a quiet country pub these days, but was once an important coaching route pit stop.

Plenty To Go Round

The other focus of village life is the excellent Brookside Cottage Shop, and seasonal Bed and Breakfast. The proprietor claims to serve a village that has a population of 20. This may be a pessimistic figure, but changing times are reflected in the two churches and three cemeteries.

The rare weeping beech in the parish churchyard seems to say it all.

There is a steep climb to Cover Head followed by a 1 in 4 descent to Kettlewell

A Spinning Stone

The 'standing stone' close to the summit of the pass features a small carved cross on one of its faces. This is locally known as the Hunter's Stone - but actually a route marker for the monks' trail between Coverham Abbey and Kettlewell. Tradition has it that the stone rotates in the ground when the clock strikes 12 at nearby Hunter's Hall.

Arkleside Moor rises starkly sources of the River Cover. The imposing fell above Kettlewell is Great Whernside.

A Jewel In The Crown

The terraced fields run down to Kettlewell - one of the exceptional jewels in the Yorkshire Dales crown.

This Anglo-Saxon settlement takes its name from a 'bubbling spring.' A market was established here in the 13th. century, but the mainstay of the economy since the middle of the 17th. century was lead mining. Most of the present buildings date from this time.

Kettlewell has a popular youth hostel. The village also possesses one of the best hostelries in the north - the Bluebell Hotel - which dates from 1680.

This famous old inn has three supernatural residents. An unidentified white lady drifts around the bedrooms. A deranged former landlord remains largely invisible but makes his presence felt by diverting beer intended for the throat - onto the lap. Finally there is a cellar poltergeist who tricks include emptying barrels at the exact moment a coach party arrives...

Follow the River Wharfe

The valley is lush and green as far as Starbottom - the last outpost reached by Anglo-Saxon settlers. Most of the buildings again date from the 17th. century. Much of the village was damaged by the worst ever flooding of the Wharfe in 1686.

Return to Buckden

Ghost Trails of the Yorkshire Dales

No. 2
Bolton
Blubberhouses
& Grassington

This circular motoring tour takes approximately nine hours

Ghost Trails of the Yorkshire Dales

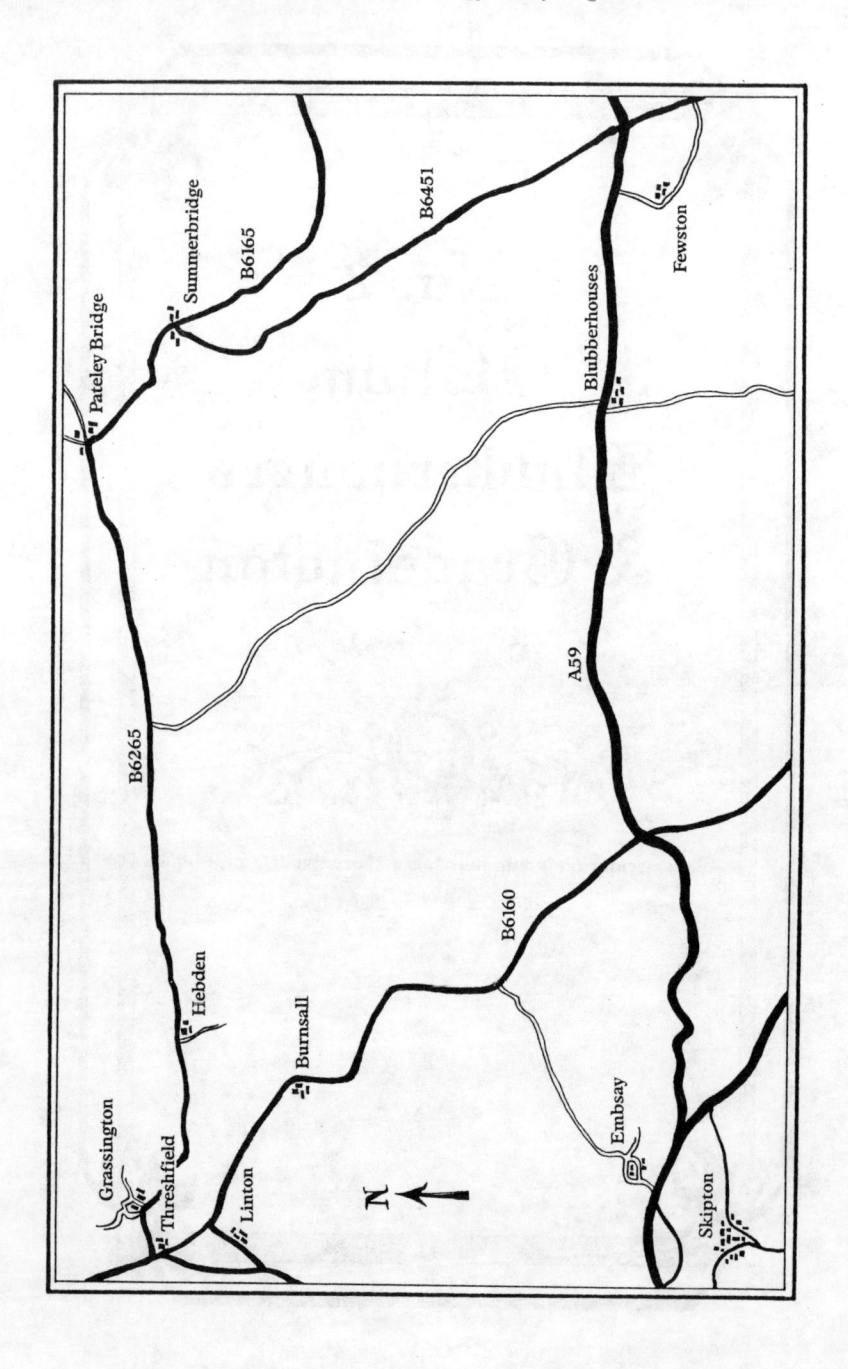

Beautiful Bolton

Park at the huge Bolton Abbey car park, and enjoy the short walk to the abbey and hall.

The setting of Bolton Abbey has made it a focus of attention for writers and artists. Ruskin and Wordsworth commended it, Landseer and Turner painted it.

Strictly speaking the abbey is a priory : the term 'abbey' refers to the village and parish.

Bolton Priory

A Brief History

In 1120 grants of land and practical assistance were arranged so that the Canons of St. Augustine could set up a modestly sized monastery. These were the Black Canons, famous for their religious discipline and strict regime.

The first community was sited at Embsay which was bleak and inhospitable. In 1154 the daughter of the founder, Alice de Rumilly, (or de Romaille) made the present site on the banks of the Wharfe available.

It is believed that some 200 people were employed directly or indirectly by the priory. A baker, brewer, cook, miller and smith provided the service back-up to the small army of builders. Beyond the precincts the priory employed farmers, herdsmen, shepherds, and foresters. Many were 'bonded men' (serfs) who received no wage.

The priory grew to become one of the most important in the north. It was attacked by Scots after Bannockburn (1314), and there was another major incursion from the north four years later. At this time the prior took refuge in Lancashire, and many of the canons escaped to the safety of Skipton Castle. The buildings were set alight and cattle and sheep were taken.

Inevitably perhaps, things were never quite the same again. By 1321 the impending visit of the archbishop was regarded with some trepidation. A lax regime had replaced the former austerity, but the friars did their best to cover up the worst excesses. It was not easy. The daily ale allowance for each friar had increased to a gallon which may explain why many neglected their devotions. There was also considerable debt, the infirmary was run-down, and some of the friars had begun to lead active sex lives.

The death of an ineffective prior lead to the re-establishment of a more disciplined regime, but the general decline was to prove terminal.

Prior Moone signed the surrender following the Pilgrimage of Grace. Clearly, some kind of deal had been negotiated. The Priory lands were returned to the Clifford estate but Prior Moone was awarded the considerable pension of £40 a year. Each of the surviving canons received £5 a year.

Today the priory is a stately ruin. Amongst many points of interest is a pre-reformation altar stone.

The Churchyard Visitor

The burial ground close to the abbey is the last resting place of many members of the Moon(e) family. In the years running up to the First World War flowers were regularly placed on some of these graves. Nobody ever saw who came to do this, and the flowers were no longer laid after the outbreak of hostilities.

Speculation at the time was that the person responsible had joined the forces. But there were also seemingly contradictory rumours that the bearer of flowers was a woman. What is certain however is that the floral tributes began again after the armistice of 1919. Again, nobody was seen.

In July 1926 a local lady died in a car crash. She had been a nurse for almost the entire duration of the war - serving mainly at a convalescence hospital near Ramsgate. Her death coincided with another break in floral deliveries to the churchyard. It may, of course, have been no more than that. She was buried in a family plot at nearby Addingham.

But once a week for the next 27 years fresh flowers were laid on her grave. Again, nobody saw the tributes arrive.

In 1953 the last flowers wilted. But just a few days earlier a sapling had been planted in the churchyard near to the grave. This was no ordinary sapling. It was a cutting from the famous Glastonbury Thorn - associated with Joseph of Arimathaea.

It may be misguided to read too much into such a tenuous list of events. Nevertheless there is a coincidence.

The lady's maiden name was Josephine Thorne.

Bolton Hall

Bolton Hall, the delightful residence of the Devonshire family, was once part of the abbey buildings. Perhaps the most obvious architectural feature is the present dining room - once a gateway to the abbey.

The resident phantom at the hall is said to be that of a servant girl. Although details of the history are contradictory, it seems likely that a son of this noble family took advantage of the girl and she died in childbirth.

The young man was sent away to live in London, but the ghost elected to haunt the hall anyway. The phantom is rarely seen, but the sound of demonic laughter, followed by the doors opening and closing, are symptoms of the manifestation.

Bolton Hall

A Gorgeous Walk

The car parking fee for Bolton Abbey also pays for the Stridd Car Park, two and a half miles away. Both are in the care of Bolton Abbey Estates. The walk from the abbey to the Stridd is delightful, and there are many possibilities for riverside picnics. A water demon is said to pull unsuspecting visitors into the Stridd Gorge, so the advice is not to go too close to the frequently fast-flowing water.

Fantastic Fewston

Join the A59 and follow the road towards Harrogate. After Blubberhouses look out for turning for Fewston. It is approximately one mile after the service station on the right.

Fewston - formerly Fuystone - was once described 'as a wild place with rude people on whose ignorance God have mercy.'

Fewston was also once known as the Moving Village because so many buildings seemed to crack and lean. This was probably the result of subsidence caused by underground watercourses, but people have also blamed the construction of the reservoirs.

Perversely it is the reservoirs that make this delightful section of the Washburn Valley so popular.

At Fewston Church turn left for the picnic area on the shores of the reservoir. The car park is also adjacent to the Swinsty Wildlife Reserve. Watch the speed stops.

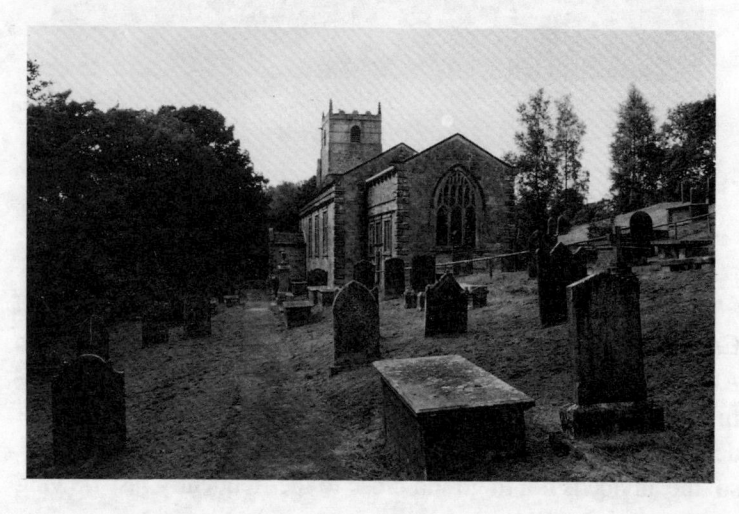

Fewston Church

The Bosky Dyke Boggart

Trees above the reservoir form part of the area (the rest is flooded) known as Bosky Dyke. This was once almost impenetrable woodland, but much of it was cleared around the turn of the 20th. century.

The woodland was the home of the famous Bosky Dyke Boggart which, according to the legend, was the ghost of a murder victim taking a terrible revenge.

Boggarts were said to be skeletal, or partly decomposed human forms. The hair was generally long and lank and the red eyes flashed wildly. A sighting was often enough to cause heart failure.

This boggart also had a repertoire of nasty tricks. These included the kind of wild shrieks that frightened horses and caused fatal accidents. He also enjoyed circling the woods in search of a lost stranger, creeping up behind, and then tapping him gently on the shoulder. In order to do this successfully the boggart had to wrap his heavy chains around his neck so that the rattling did not give warning of his approach.

Happily it seems the boggart disappeared with the woodland. But a late Victorian poem reminds us of his reputation :

Long tales are told from sire to son
In many a forest ingle
Of rushing sounds and fearful sights
In Bosky Dyke's dark dingle.

Where thickest fell the gloom of night
And terror held its sway,
Now beams the rising son of light
And intellectual day.

But whereupon in former times
Was fear for man and beast,
The cutting of the woodland swathe

The boggart has released.

Yet softly tread,with reverent step
Along the Bosky shade
Where ghosts our forebears feared of old
Will be forever laid.

Return to the church

A Vanishing Village

Fewston certainly sparks the imagination. There are shadows of the past everywhere, but relatively little of substance is left to reflect glory days.

The church was once at the head of a street of densely packed houses that lead all the way down to the river. There was a bakery, a smithy, and a popular hostelry opposite the north gate of the churchyard.

Impossible Dates

Fewston's lovely parish church is dedicated to St. Michael and St. Lawrence. There are fine box tombs in the churchyard. One marks the grave of Joseph Ridsdale who died on 29th. February 1823, and one of his sons who died on 30th. February 1802. Both are impossible dates.

A Mysterious Death

Another stone tells a tragic story. A 15 year old boy, Joseph Wood, had taken a cow to Otley. His family became concerned when he did not return and the villagers turned out to search. The boy was found dead, but the bovine and canine companions had loyally remained close to the body. The cause of death is unknown.

Fires Over Fewston

The church has twice been ravaged by fire, most recently in 1696. The stone over the doorway commemorates the completion of the new building the following year.

An Architectural Rarity

This is a rare example of a 17th. century church built on the medieval model. It suggests the sturdy traditionalism of Yorkshire folk.

Inside the building there is an ornate spiral staircase that leads to the unusual first floor bell ringing chamber.

At some stage the font had an extra piece added, and the cover was simply too low and heavy to be manoeuvred by hand. The engineered solution to this is the distinctive gallows hoist.

A board lists the rectors of Fewston from the early 13th. century. This was a large parish where the rector was an important man. He organised the work of a number of curates who shared pastoral responsibility on a day-to-day basis.

The Witch Trails

The rector at the time of Fewston's most celebrated moment in history was Nicholas Smythson.

He was said to be a quiet man of exceptional piety, who did not welcome the spotlight of publicity. But the role he was to play in the events of 1621 and 1622 proved critical.

The other leading player in the drama was Edward Fairfax of New Hall. His account of events was published as the 'Discourse on Witchcraft as it was acted in the family of Edward Fairfax of Fuystone in the County of York in the Year AD 1621.'

The book strains credulity today. But King James I himself had given the seal of approval to the witch hunts, and the hysteria did not die until the last witch was tried more than a century later.

Edward Fairfax was a rational man who tried to make sense of the terrible tragedies that beset his family. But as he became obsessive, his rationality began to evaporate. Finally he was motivated mainly by revenge.

His 'Discourse on Witchcraft' talks of spells and magic acted on his daughters - Ellen, Ann, and Elizabeth. The account begins in October 28th. 1621 when Ellen was found lying on the parlour floor 'in a deadly trance.' The girl recovered, but was afflicted a second time several days later.

The medical advice offered was not helpful : 'The maladie is an afflication of the brain, by what cause or agent we know not.'

The attacks continued and the girl became weaker. Then Elizabeth began to display similar symptoms.

Edward Fairfax sat at the bedside of the girls as they were semi-conscious. He kept a log of their ramblings. Though the words he recorded were often incoherent and even contradictory, Fairfax claimed they were insights.

He named six local women as witches. Their ringleader, - Margaret Thorp, was dragged from her bed to the parish church and instructed to say the Lord's Prayer. She stumbled over the words 'forgive us our trespasses'. For Fairfax, this was sufficient proof of witchery.

But the rector, Nicholas Smythson, was concerned. He was not convinced by the accusations. However he recognised that a challenge to Fewston's wealthiest and most influential man would be damaging not only to himself, but to the parish.

The women were tried at York. The judges were told how the coven met at Timble Gill Beck. The precise location was recorded as a 'fairy bridge' close to the place where the stream enters the Washburn river.

All three of the Fairfax girls died. Ann had suffered the same terrible convulsions as Ellen. Elizabeth had seemed to recover, but had suffered fatal injuries after falling from a haystack.

The evidence against the women was fragmentary and bizarre. Bess Foster was accused of casting the fatal spell on Elizabeth. Margaret Waite was accused of making a 'terrible curse with a stolen pennyworth of corn.' Margaret Thorp was accused of making pictures of the girls and 'casting them into the water.' Janet Dibb was named as coven cook with 'recipes 'so foul as to tempt Lucifer himself to the feasting.' All the women were accused of 'carrying the children to the hilltop to see the midsummer bonfire.'

When the case against the women began to collapse, Edward Fairfax brought fresh 'evidence.' The unfortunate 'witches' found themselves thrown back into prison whilst preparations were made for a second trial.

But Nicholas Smythson intervened. There was growing disquiet in the parish. Indeed, the stakes in the game were getting dangerously high and the rector had to show his hand. He organised defence petitions that lead to the women's acquittal.

The story is that the 'Fewston Witches' celebrated their return with a massive banquet. It is not known if Edward Fairfax was invited. The rector certainly declined. Perhaps this was prudent. After all, the story goes that Lucifer himself was the Guest of Honour.

Edward Fairfax is buried in the churchyard at Fewston and the remains of his residence, New Hall, have long since disappeared beneath the water. But the 'Discourse on Witchcraft' is in many ways his true memorial. It has become fashionable to mock this account of events, but the document is a considerable aid to understanding the thinking and beliefs of 17th. century. Furthermore, the case Fairfax made for 'proving' witchcraft is not too far removed from the thinking of a famous fictional detective who 'lived' two centuries later : 'When you have eliminated the impossible, whatever remains, however improbable, must be the truth.'

Murder At The Fairy Bridge

The 'Fairy Bridge' was also the site of a murder.

On a July day in 1657 a weary traveller was taking his rest by the waterside when he was set upon by a gang of poachers. They robbed him, beat him with heavy sticks, and left him for dead.

The unfortunate man awoke from unconsciousness, and in great pain managed to crawl as far as the roadway. He collapsed, but was found in a semi-delirious state by a group of children.

One of the youngsters went for help, but his story was not immediately believed. By the time help arrived the traveller was dead, but during his final moments he had described his attackers to the other children.

They were interviewed by the magistrate and recalled that one of the murderous gang had blackened teeth and a pock-marked face. This description pointed the finger of suspicion at Joab Skelton - a notorious rogue from Blubberhouses. He was brought in to face the justice's inquisition, and his property was searched. The most damning piece of evidence was a blood-stained shirt, but Skelton insisted that this was the result of skinning a rabbit.

No formal charges were brought against him. This is probably because the youngster's second-hand account of the attack would have been problematic as evidence, and to nobody's great surprise Skelton's friends provided him with an alibi.

A Strange Shape

At a certain point, as the road winds down towards the waterside, an odd phenomenon has been noticed. An ever-changing shape, but not perhaps unlike that of a man, seems to hover in the air. The form is sometimes faint and translucent; sometimes quite solid and threatening.

Could this be a trick of the light? The flickering of pale sunshine through the branches perhaps? The imagination can perform some mischief, particularly when you know that this is the very place where a man once died.

The man was Joab Skelton. He met his end as the victim of a trap set for a different kind of animal. The howling of the winter's gale was enough to drown the frenzy of his cries for help. When he was found his pock-marked features were twisted into lines of unspeakable agony. His bottom lip had been almost completely severed by his own teeth.

In Fewston they called it 'The Traveller's Justice.'

The George Eliot Connection

In 1859 the Reverend John Gwyther wrote a letter to the publisher of George Eliot's 'Scenes of Clerical Life'.

The Reverend Gwyther was sure that one of the stories in the collection - 'The Sad Fortunes of the Reverend Amos Barton'- was based on an episode in his own life.

'I find it unkind,' he wrote,'taking such a great liberty with a living character.'

The publisher admitted the connection, but pointed out that the author had based the story on events so far in the past that 'she was under the impression that the clergyman was no longer living.' An apology was added.

George Eliot's story tells of the relationship between a widowed Polish countess, her brother, and the Reverend Barton and his wife. As the plot unfolds we find the Reverend Barton at odds with his parishioners, and in constant dispute about rents and taxes. Finally, he leaves the Midlands with six motherless children and begins a new life in the north.

The writer had created her storyline from newspaper reports of real events that occurred in a parish near Nuneaton. The model for Amos Barton was John Gwyther, and the characterisation (though invented) was also uncannily accurate. In both fact and fiction the man was hardworking and well-intentioned, but wildly intolerant and tactless.

He became Vicar of Fewston in 1844. The Midlands parish he left behind was in disarray, and his personal life was in turmoil.

The continuing saga of his life at Fewston could easily be read as Amos Barton 2. Three of the children of his first marriage died young. He married again and had two further sons, but the silver linings on the Gwyther horizon were blotted out when his young wife died giving birth to a daughter. The infant died a few days later.

John Gwyther was respected, but almost universally unpopular. He fell out with leading parishioners, and became embroiled in further financial disputes.

A letter he wrote in 1849 to his curate is almost pure George Eliot. He instructed the young man: 'Your domiciliary visitations should be more frequent. I consider them absolutely necessary for carrying out a system of parochial instruction to my satisfaction.'

John Gwyther died in 1873. A large tombstone near the church porch records his tenure at Fewston rather more diplomatically: 'This tomb is erected in affectionate remembrance of his ministerial labours by a large number of his parishioners.'

The Village Shop Murder

The horrific incident in 1938 still leaves many unanswered questions.

At ten o'clock one sunny morning a customer entered the small village shop. It was quiet and dark inside, and at first the customer did not take in the full horror of the vision before her.

On the floor was the badly beaten body of the shopkeeper, Margaret Peel. Blood had splattered and stained a wide area of the floor, shelves and walls.

Margaret's husband, Jesse, was brought home from his job at Swinsty reservoir. He behaved oddly. The first thing he did was to check the till, stepping around his wife's body almost without looking.

Some of Jesse's unwashed clothing was bloodstained. He claimed that he had cut himself on a briar.

The evidence against him was entirely circumstantial. A possible murder weapon - a tyre lever - was found near the edge of the reservoir, but there was nothing to positively link this to Jesse. Nor was there any suggestion that Jesse Peel had ever had a major disagreement with his wife.

But there were no other suspects. Jesse was tried and acquitted. Many people thought that the trial should never have taken place. Couldn't his odd behaviour easily be explained by the shock of his wife's brutal death?

It seems likely that the murderer was an opportunist thief who found Margaret Peel rather more sturdy opposition than expected. Panic followed the killing, and escape without detection became more important than the change in the till.

Jesse Peel died in a road accident in 1942.

Ghost Trails of the Yorkshire Dales

Take the minor road to Timble. Turn sharp left at the road junction and park near to the Timble Inn

The ghost of a retired sea captain, once a regular at the inn, is said to appear only at times of National crisis.

A National Disaster?

His last 'official' visit was on the eve of the declaration of hostilities in 1939, although there is a tentative sighting in November 1993. This may be scurrilous. The only event of National significance on the date in question was England's humiliating elimination from the World Cup.

Timble Inn

The Swinsty Spooks

The 16th. century Swinsty Hall is situated at the end of a track near the reservoir.

In the 1970's the Cuckston family felt the presence of ghosts.

Mrs Cuckston was in the basement kitchen one day when she heard a voice saying 'hello.' She believed she was alone in the house - except for her young daughter who was eating her dinner. She dashed upstairs to greet the visitor. There was nobody there.

The phantom voice also disturbed Mr. Cuckston, who has answered it only to find he too was alone.

An even odder experience for Mrs Cuckston was when she believed her husband had followed her to bed one night. She woke up to find the light on, the bed beside her empty, and her husband still downstairs listening to music.

On another occasion Mrs Cuckston placed the new born baby in a crib near to her own bed. She awoke feeling cold, but settled down again as a blanket was placed over her.

In the morning she remembered to thank her husband. He had been up late, and had opted to sleep in another room to avoid disturbing his wife and child.

He had not entered their bedroom.

The Cobbler's Tale

Another strange Timble tale relates to events of 1825.

The local cobbler, Will Holmes, rented a house and workshop.

One day he entered his workshop to find an old glue tin filled with pairings and scraps. At the top of the pile there was a small leather cross.

Will decided that this was a joke - probably perpetrated by some of the village lads. That night he locked his doors and shutters, and as an extra precaution, he balanced the tin on a iron rod. Even the faintest vibration would cause it to fall.

The tin was filled again the next morning and the leather cross was in place.

Will's next move was to sweep up every scrap of waste material and to burn it. The following morning the tin was full again - this time with broken glass and wood, plus the leather cross.

He decided to consult the vicar. Both waited outside the workshop after dark. They heard shuffling and breathing noises but were frightened to enter.

In the morning the tin was full again.

This was enough for Will. Although the tin was only ever part filled on one further occasion, he had made up his mind. He quit the cobbling business and went into farming.

Will Holmes always believed that he had been victimised by the spirit of Tommy Kaye, 'the village idiot', who had died some months earlier.

Retrace your route briefly. Follow the Otley sign at the crossroads, then follow Blubberhouses and Pateley Bridge. Turn right at the A59, then first left. From Blubberhouses take the C road link to the B6265 west of Pateley Bridge.

All In The Game

The wild location of Blubberhouses Cricket Club proves the passion for the game in Yorkshire. Summer in these parts is said to last for up to three weeks in a good year.

The upland area rises to just over 1300 feet at Brown Bank Head. The Washburn rises to the north on the splendidly named Pockstones Moor. This is marsh country whose main residents appear to be woolly coated cattle.

Still Roman Around

A phantom troop of Roman soldiers is said to wander eternally around the moor. There seems to be no certain historical precedent for this. However there is some evidence that points to a possible scenario.

Following the defeat of Venutius at Stanwick in 79 AD, one of the retreating Brigantian tribes found a safe haven on these moors. The Roman method of pacification is well known, and it is not unlikely that a patrol was sent to check out the remnants of the opposition.

Some say that the patrol was massacred, but it is perhaps as likely that the men were victims of exposure.

One of the most recent sightings was in August 1983. Martin Yates and Steve Allan were graduate students with an interest in Mesolithic artifacts. They were working in a narrow trench when they heard what both described as raised and angry voices.

Martin takes up the story.

"We both looked up at the same time," he says, "and saw a group of a dozen figures above us on Barden Fell. It was difficult to make out much detail but it's clear there was some sort of scuffle.

" I dug into the rucksack for the binoculars. When you're in a hurry nothing ever comes to hand quickly. I had to empty everything else before I found them. I lifted the glasses and focused. I couldn't believe it. I was watching a detachment of Roman infantrymen.

" The disagreement was now ended. The soldiers were walking steadily in a line towards the top of the hill. The space between each of the men was about the same, except for the man at the back who looked as if he was struggling to keep up. I could even see the wet mud clinging to his tunic. If there'd been a fight, I was looking at the loser.

" I passed the glasses to Steve. He didn't believe what he was seeing either. We watched for more than five minutes. Finally they moved out of our sight.

" We thought of the logical explanations. Was somebody making a film? Could it be one of those groups who dress up to recreate a moment in history?

" We asked questions. But it was only then we heard the Lost Patrol story that it all began to add up. It wasn't scary, and neither of us considered the supernatural at the time. We'd been watching a real event. It's just that it happened nearly 2000 years ago..."

Join the B6265 and turn left towards Grassington

An Underground Wonderland

The famous Stump Cross Caverns were discovered by lead miners in 1858.

The carboniferous limestone is particularly good for forming the magnificent stalactites and stalagmites. The caverns also feature spectacular rimstone pools.

Stump Cross is a deservedly popular show cave. The full system runs for three and a half miles. The visitor is treated to a restricted, but rewarding, one third of a mile. Imaginative lighting makes this a highly recommended tour. The cafe is also noted as one of the best in the Dales.

Clogged Up

Phantom footsteps are frequently heard echoing around the caverns but the ghost remains elusive and invisible.

Visitors are often told that the sound is made by the clogs of a former mine worker. Certainly the strange but distinctive sound has been heard frequently for more than a century. It seems as if the phantom miner is doomed never the escape the caverns.

Turn left off the B6285 towards Appletreewick, Burnsall, and Parcevall Hall.

Troller's Gate

The narrow road to Parcevall Hall passes a field gate on the left before it crosses a wooden bridge. The path from this gate leads upwards towards Troller's Gill. The fingerpost indicates 'Gill Head'.

This is a slate mining area. The walk is worthwhile but should only be attempted by the more active. A sturdy pair of boots is recommended.

The Barguest

Troller's Gill is sometimes associated with trolls, but its real notoriety comes from something much more terrible.

It was a certain Mr. Troller who earned posthumous fame by coming second in a battle with the barguest. The name of this 'mountain demon' derives from the Germanic Saxon - Bergeist. Other possible spellings include bierguest, bargest, bahrgeist and boguest. The last of these forms a vernacular link with boggart.

But barguest and boggart are distinctly different. Where Barguest is animal, boggart is human. The appearance of this terrible creature is said to foretell death.

This particular barguest was described as a giant shaggy-coated dog with red rolling saucer eyes. His preferred diet was said to be well- rotted human flesh, which may begin to explain his chronic halitosis. It is generally believed that barguests dislike water.

For the Troller's Gill barguest this was clearly a fully fledged anathema. The smell he generated was enough to induce reflex vomiting at short range, and could create a general feeling of nausea at distances of several hundred metres. Much, of course, depended on the direction of the breeze.

The distinctive barguest aroma served as a useful early warning system. But, if nasal sensitivity was substandard the barguest was at least sporting enough to provide a second warning of his presence. He wore a redundant necklace with additional loops of chain that dangled and crashed on the ground. The necklace was not an uncharacteristic vanity. It was the legacy of an ill-judged attempt to capture the beast.

It is said that Mr. Troller fell from his horse whilst attempting to navigate the gorge at midnight. His disorientation may have resulted from the fall, but is more likely to be linked to his three hour stay at a local hostelry. Certainly he made a fatal mistake. Rather than walking directly towards the road, he turned around and wandered back into the depths of the gorge.

The body was found by shepherds. He was lying under a yew tree. Those who saw the corpse remarked that the face was frozen in horror. There was something else too. He seemed to have been part crushed by an enormous weight. The worst marks were 'impressed deep into the chest, and seemed not to be made by mortal hand.'

He was buried in Burnsall churchyard.

There is also a story of a more wily adversary for the barguest.

A farmer heard the rattle of chain in the darkness, and guessed that the fearsome creature was looking for his supper. The man moved carefully, stopping to listen from time to time, and now and then catching a glimpse of the terrible flashing eyes. He was also by now well aware of the barguest's approach to personal hygiene.

By using his knowledge of the terrain the farmer was able to manoeuvre his position so that water was constantly between himself and his predator. Gradually he eased himself further away from the barguest before leaping a second stream and making his escape.

Abandoned

Simon's Seat is formed by group of rocks north of Barden Fell. Dales chronicler, Halliwell Sutcliffe, tells the story of a baby abandoned here.

The child was found by a shepherd called Simon. When the search for the mother of the child failed, the child was also given the name Simon. He was brought up by the shepherding community and became an honorary member of several local families. Because of this unusual arrangement the boy earned the name Simon Amangham - dialect for 'among them'.

Follow the narrow road to Parcevall Hall. There is a tricky left turn on the approach to the hall. The lovely grounds are open to the public from Easter to October.

The Parson's Hall

This was once literally the Parson's Hall - named after the wealthy Reverend Haye. The present spelling of Parcevall has been derived via Parsible and Parsifal. The house is now used as a retreat for the Diocese of Bradford.

The Family Way

The end of the building is called the 'Bride House.' These apartments were traditionally given to heir and his wife. This was said to ensure a male heir, and for at least six generations it seemed to do the trick.

This may have been coincidence. There are longstanding local claims that aconite (Monkshood) has the same effect, with the added bonus of certain aphrodisiac qualities.

The rhizomes of the plant were cleaned, sliced and heated before dry storage. This had to be thoroughly watertight because even the smallest amount of liquid could release poisonous alkaloids.

At the end of the 17th. century Dales diarist William Pierce wrote:

' Aconite was taken in honey by the brides of Parcevall. This is the very exposition of begetting male heirs. Aconite is much vaunted in these parts also (as a) remedy for ague and rheumatics.'

Haunted Horses?

The Parcevall stables are said to be haunted, but there seem to be few accounts of supernatural events.

It seems that on several occasions the horses were found to be shivering and terrified for no obvious reason, but clues do come from two incomplete stories.

A local legend is that the heir to the estate fell for the ample charms of an innkeeper's daughter. For some time all went well. She would visit the hall and they would take out horses before returning to his apartments for exercise of a more intimate kind.

After a while she became less enthusiastic about the second half of these fixtures, but retained her passion for the horses.

Inevitably this lead to an argument. Unwisely perhaps she declared that the real object of her desire was the young man who looked after the stables.

This was an affront to the Parcevall heir who promptly beat the young ostler to death.

The story ends here, without any account of the hauntings or the fate of the heir and the innkeeper's daughter.

A better reason for the equine alarms was offered by William Pierce. His account explains : 'A certain man was guardian of the stables. He was charged to feague the animals, but this he declined (to do). The mistress was greatly displeased and ordered servants to whip the recalcitrant ostler. They came to the stable, but upon the raising of the whip one beast kicked out with such a blow as to make the fellow (with the whip) insensible. The ostler took flight. He did not return to the parish. The servant recovered but the master was not pleased. He (the servant) was confined to the labour of the stables.'

This demands explanation. The practice of feaguing has now hopefully died out, though an etymological link is clear in the expression 'ginger up.'

This involved 'putting ginger or inserting objects into a horse's rectum to make it hold up its tail.' Naturally enough this did not always delight the horse. The presence of a whip may also have created equine anxiety. Indeed Pierce's story suggests several reasons why the horses should show serious symptoms of panic - particularly when placed in the 'care' of the newly demoted servant.

The Victorian ghost hunter, Alfred Dunn, believed that Pierce's 'explanation' was part of a cover-up for the crime. Although Pierce's account is contemporary, Dunn argued that Pierce had digested the 'authorised' version. The ostler 'not returning to the parish' was a convenient way of closing the book on a murder. Dunn also suggested that the Pierce account made little sense. In the 17th. century the feague was a matter of fashion, and even perhaps routine. So why should the ostler refuse to do it?

Alfred Dunn was also disappointed by his vigil at the stable.

'I waited in great anticipation,' he wrote, ' and considered perhaps that I heard something or felt a chilling presence. But I cannot say it was more than my fancy. If there is a tormented spirit here I did not detect it.'

Return along the C road and follow the signs to Appletreewick Appletreewick, one of the 'Jewels of the Dales' was once noted for its Onion Fair.

A Fearsome Phantom

17th. century Low Hall is near to the Craven Arms. The hall was once the home of Thomas Preston whose 'grisly spectre terrorised Wharfedale with bangs, groans and yells.'

The reason for the haunting is unclear. It is said that a priest exorcized the ghost at a place in Dibb Gill, now known as Preston's Well.

In High Spirits

Another ghost haunted the lane beyond the village for many years. This spectre was finally confronted by a local man who showed how much courage could be gained by an extended visit to a public house.

The man demanded to know the reason for the haunting. The reply was an unlikely one.

The unfortunate spectre confessed to moving a neighbour's landmark boulders to gain an extra strip of land. Filled with remorse he bought poison and committed suicide.

The drunk promised to replace the boulders and pay the chemist for the poison. The ghost vanished and was never seen again.

Notorious Nick

The Jacobean High Hall was once the home of a magistrate who could be persuaded to turn a blind eye to certain wrongdoings.

It is said that the highwayman, Nick Nevinson, stayed here on a number of occasions. Where better to hide from his pursuers than the home of a respected magistrate?

Nick Nevinson is the strongest candidate for the record-breaking ride from London to York that became associated with Dick Turpin through the Harrison Ainsworth novel 'Rockwood'.

Nick Nevinson had a most successful career : it is said he was responsible for more than 1000 robberies. He has therefore a strong claim to the title 'King of the Highwaymen.'

First Lord Of London

The chapel opposite High Hall used to be cottages. This was the birthplace of William Craven, the Yorkshire 'Dick Whittington'.

William's origins were humble enough, nor did he demonstrate great scholastic ability as a pupil at Burnsall Grammar School.

But William left for London, and, after struggling for a living, found a post with the banker, Robert Hulson. In an even better career move he married Hulson's daughter and took over a financial empire.

In 1610 - just half a dozen years after leaving Yorkshire - William became Lord Mayor and High Sheriff of London. His career developed further through cultivating friends in high places. These included members of the Royal Family, and most particularly Elizabeth of Bohemia, the sister of Charles I. Princess Elizabeth, also known as the Winter Queen and the Queen of Hearts, had 'stunned the court with her beauty' when she made her debut appearance in 1608. It is said that William Craven, though far too lowly in rank to be a serious suitor, 'enjoyed the Queen's affection throughout her days.'

During the Civil War he fell from grace. The Restoration brought further high office and honours, and the association with Elizabeth of Bohemia was renewed when she returned from exile in Holland. It is said that William was instrumental in shaking the moths from the wallet of Charles II to ensure she received a suitable pension.

The plague forced the court out of London in 1665 and William Craven became Governor of the City. He was also important to the rebuilding process that followed the Great Fire of 1666.

In the course of his career William Craven became famously wealthy, but he was also a generous man. He gave many important endowments to the district of his birth.

The present High Hall was created for the Craven Family, who centuries later gave the cottages opposite to the people of Appletreewick to be used as a Chapel of Ease.

The lovely little chapel maintains a traditional link with the 17th. century. It is only place of worship in the diocese that retains the 1662 prayer book for all services. The citizens of Appletreewick should be justifiably proud of this splendid stubbornness.

Mock Beggar Hall

This fine old building was once linked to Bolton Abbey. It is thought the name derives from a special hole or hatchway that was used to pass out food to the poor.

World Beer Centre

The New Inn has sometimes been claimed as the 'World Beer Centre.' Whilst perhaps Milwaukee and Munich, amongst others, may dispute this title, the inn has earned a reputation for providing just about the largest range of ales in the UK under one roof.

The added bonus is that this is proper beer, as opposed to the pale gassy stuff known as lager.

A Friendly Phantom?

Locals claim that an unusual phantom stalks footpaths above the village. Strangers in particular have often found themselves joined by a friendly companion who vanishes as suddenly as he appears.

The 'phantom' seems able to take on a number of guises - from elderly farmer to teenage hiker. As with similar phenomena this 'phantom' is most frequently encountered in misty conditions...

Follow the C road to Burnsall

The First Fell Race

Burnsall takes its name from the Saxon Brineshale. The village has a famous feast and sports day in August. Centre stage at the sports is the classic fell race - probably the longest established event of its kind in the UK - which dates from the reign of the first Queen Elizabeth.

Ancient And Modern

The old Grammar School (now a primary school) was founded in 1602. It is said that William Craven was one of the 'foundation' pupils. He was later to become the school's greatest benefactor. The building features lovely mullioned windows, but more modern times are reflected in a playground marked for hopscotch and netball.

The former Grammer School, Burnsall

Earliest Christian Site

St. Wilfred's Parish Church has claims to be the oldest site of Christianity in the Dales. Tradition has it that St. Wilfred preached from a rock in the Wharfe and founded a wooden church on the present site in the late 7th. century.

The stone building was begun by Alice de Romaille in 1140. 'Repairs and beautification were paid for from the Craven purse in 1612. The church features the remains of Saxon crosses, a Saxon font, and an Italian 'Adoration of the Magi' from the middle of the 14th. century. The church also contains a rather fine example of the traditional coffin carriage.

A board in the church lists the rectors from 1270. The earliest were John de Kyrkaby and William de Reddemere - who each presided over a 'mediaty' or part of the parish. The arrangement was not unusual in large rural parishes.

The churchyard stocks are apparently in their original position. They are close to the final resting place of William Bolton, better known as the Dales Minstrel.

The Dales Minstrel

William Bolton was an itinerant knife-sharpener who was also an excellent fiddler. Despite his popularity he died a pauper. A local collection was taken to provider him with a grave and headstone.

Two Eccentric Vicars

St. Wilfred's had two eccentric vicars - both called John Adcott.

The first forgot his sermon notes and read instead from the bible, claiming the good book was worth ten sermons. On another occasion a mischievous parishioner mixed up the order of the sermon notes. The Reverend Adcott delivered it without rearranging the order, and invited the congregation 'to make what sense of it they would.'

At a wedding ceremony the same Reverend Adcott was confronted with a strong-minded Yorkshire lass who refused to acknowledge the oath of

Memorial to Dales Minstrel, William Bolton

obedience. The reverend hesitated for a moment, then continued with the service as though nothing had happened.

The second John Adcott was a gentle bumbling character prone to the unfortunate combination of Spoonerism and stammering. Before his appointment to St. Wilfreds he had been tutor to Eugene Aram - the notorious Knaresborugh murderer.

The Thistle Hill Murder

Following the tuition of John Adcott, Eugene Aram became a teacher in Nidderdale in 1714.

The hunt for a killer began when workmen uncovered a badly decomposed corpse at Thistle Hill in Knaresborough. There was evidence to suggest that this was the body of Daniel Clark who has disappeared 14 years earlier.

Eugene Aram was the prime suspect because of well-founded speculation that he had been involved with Clark in some dodgy deals. Daniel Clark himself had earned the reputation of a highly skilled con-artist.

The evidence against Aram was at best circumstantial, but then a third man - Richard Houseman - turned King's Evidence. This was enough to seal Eugene Aram's fate. He even admitted the crime after his conviction.

Aram was hung at York and the body was gibbeted in Knaresborough Forest. For a while the edifying spectacle of putrefying flesh became something of a tourist attraction, but interest declined as the birds picked back to the whiteness of the bone.

Nevertheless there was some local anger when the skeleton disappeared. In order to preserve at least a minor macabre relic, the landlord of the Brewer's Arms won permission to remove the remains of the gibbet. This was used to replace a rotted beam in the Knaresborough hostelry.

Moonlight Dancing

A popular local story tells of an inebriate farmer's encounter with the Burnsall fairies.

It seems that the man was on his way home one night in the customary state of intoxication when he encountered the fairies dancing in the moonlight.

The farmer decided to join in the festivities by singing the verses he could remember of 'Ilkla Moor Bah't'at'. The fairies were clearly displeased by this musical contribution because they invited him to shut up. When he refused they attacked him. He staggered and fell as the blows rained down from all angles.

When he lay flat out in the mud the Fairy Queen gave the order to end the attack.

The farmer woke some hours later and dragged himself to his feet. As he lurched along the lane he reached in his pocket for a handkerchief. He was about to mop his injured face when he felt a small lump in the cloth. He opened it to find a fairy curled up and asleep. Carefully he returned the handkerchief to its place.

When he arrived home his wife demanded to know what had occurred.

He told her all about the fairies, and produced the handkerchief as certain proof. But the sleeping fairy had made an escape, and the unfortunate farmer was forced to do the same as his wife approached him with a menacingly held rolling pin...

The Mobile Maypole

The Burnsall maypole is sited on the green in the same position as the one that was once stolen by a 'raiding party' from nearby Thorpe-sub-Montem. This sparked a feud between the villages which was only ended by the return of the pole.

Burnsall's green is a lovely place to spend a summer's afternoon, with the excellent Red Lion Hotel conveniently sited for the necessary refreshments. The views of the fells are as fine as you will find, and the peaty waters of Wharfe are ideal for cooling the weary ghost trailer's feet.

Claims To Fame

Burnsall offers other historical curiosities. There are three holy wells. One of these - Thor's Well - indicates both Viking and pagan associations.

In more recent times a local farmer's daughter grew up to marry, move, and become the mother of England's greatest naval hero - Horatio Nelson.

A Strange Spectre

On winter evenings a lonely figure has often been seen walking in Burnsall. He appears to be a small man, made yet smaller in appearance because of his hunched shoulders and hunched back. The figure wears the familiar breeches and top coat and hat of the early Victorian gentleman farmer.

Those who approach closely notice something else. As the head is slowly raised vacant orbs of a skeletal face transmit a chilling greeting. Some courageous observers have also remarked on the way the blackness of the teeth is accentuated by the milky whiteness of a drooping jaw bone.

But nobody can come too close to this figure. Almost as soon as the full horror of the spectacle has registered on observers, it fades into the ether.

This grisly apparition was encountered in 1992 by Marie and Therese Prevost, who had otherwise enjoyed a peaceful and enjoyable hostelling holiday in the Dales. There is no doubt of the most vivid memory that they took home to the Auvergne.

There were two similar recorded sightings in the 1980's. In ghost-trailing terms this is a most singular phenomenon as there are no earlier accounts of sightings.

The spectre has not been identified, but there has been speculation that this could be the ghost of Thomas Denholme, a farmer of agoraphobic and miserly instincts, whose emaciated body was found several months after his death in 1842. But if this is the case, it is difficult to understand why the ghost should wait for a century and a half before making his presence felt.

The road to Bolton Abbey follows the Wharfe. There are fine views over the river to Appletreewick.

A Famous Ruin

Barden Tower is well worth a visit. The ruins are open to the public during daylight hours. The adjacent building is the Priest's House - now in the Premier League of Dales tea-rooms.

Barden Tower

The tower was originally a 12th. century hunting lodge, but the building is largely associated with the Clifford family who rebuilt and developed it. The inscription over the entrance reminds us that Lady Anne Clifford carried out many of the repairs (1658/59) and that her mother stayed here before Lady Anne's birth.

A Colourful Clifford

Henry Clifford is the most colourful character associated with the tower.

Seven year old Henry went into hiding with his mother after the Battle of Towton (near Tadcaster). This infamous battle, was fought in a snowstorm on Palm Sunday 1461.

Towton was the most decisive battle of the Wars of the Roses, and with up to 60,000 combatants, is probably the largest ever fought in the UK. Fierce fighting carried on throughout the day, and estimates of casualties (perhaps 12,000) suggest that Towton edges out Flodden for the right to be called the bloodiest battle on British soil. There were acres of red snow on the ground, and when the melt came blood flowed down the Cork Beck to the Wharfe - which remained visibly red as far as the junction with the Ouse.

After this carnage Edward IV was briefly the undisputed master of England.

Henry's father, who died at Towton, was characterised as 'Black Clifford' by Shakespeare. This was a propagandist interpretation in keeping with Tudor historical orthodoxy.

Young Henry was hidden by his mother with a shepherd's family at Threlkeld in the Lake District. The shepherd worked on the estate of a friend of the family. The boy was encouraged to forget his past, and it was 24 years before (after Bosworth) he was able to reclaim his estates and take his place as the Lord of Skipton Castle.

Henry began his new life as an illiterate lord, but with the courage to take his yokel clothes and Cumberland accent to the House of Lords. Indeed, he never lost the accent or common touch, but took so enthusiastically to education that he became an acknowledged expert in astronomy, chemistry and physics.

He fought alongside the Earl of Surrey at Flodden (1513) and became an advisor to the young King Henry VIII. He restored Barden Tower, and his generosity to the poor and dispossessed earned him the name 'Good Lord Clifford.' Henry survived into his eighth decade. He was buried in the choir at Bolton Priory.

A Wicked Clifford

Henry's son, the first Earl of Cumberland, was a less saintly character. Although it is perhaps unfair to suggest that Henry's title (granted in 1525) was earned through enthusiastic service as 'procurer of wenches' to Henry VIII, there may well be an element of truth in this.

Indeed, the young earl had remarkable sexual appetites - even by the standards of his day. His work as 'procurer' to the king demanded sampling, cataloguing, and the making of clandestine arrangements. His off-duty pastimes included gluttony, alcoholism, and an imaginative repertoire of sadistic practices.

He remained fiercely loyal to the king, and threw himself enthusiastically into the task of stamping out the insurrections in the north. One fringe benefit of all this were the many opportunities that arose for the ransacking and pillaging of monasteries.

Henry grew rather rich, but also corpulent and pig-eyed. A respiratory complaint overtook the progress of certain anti-social diseases to end his days prematurely in 1542.

A Grisly Find

Although perhaps unconnected with the 1st. Earl, the terrible death of two boys men in 1537 has often been laid at his door.

The bodies were found in a field less than a mile from Barden Tower. They were found stripped an 'strangely mutilated'. The obvious injuries included many marks of the lash, crushed thumbs, and fractures at the elbow and knee. There was inevitable speculation of torture, and it does seem likely that the unfortunate victims were racked and broken on the wheel.

Even in times when life regularly ended brutally, the age of these boys - both around ten years - was enough to cause a furore. The identity of the youngsters was never clearly established, though one source has it they were 'brought from Embsay.'

A Scream In The Dark

Barden Tower fell rapidly into ruin after the lead and timbers were taken in the 1780's. But whilst the building was more or less complete, a single echoing scream was often heard from within the walls.

The anguished note of the voice was high, and it is said this 'oftimes chilled the blood of travellers.' The locals accepted it more as a matter of routine. They called it ' the shout from hell.

Return to Bolton Abbey

No. 3
Nidderdale, Ripon & Fountains Abbey

This circular motoring tour takes approximately eight hours

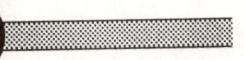

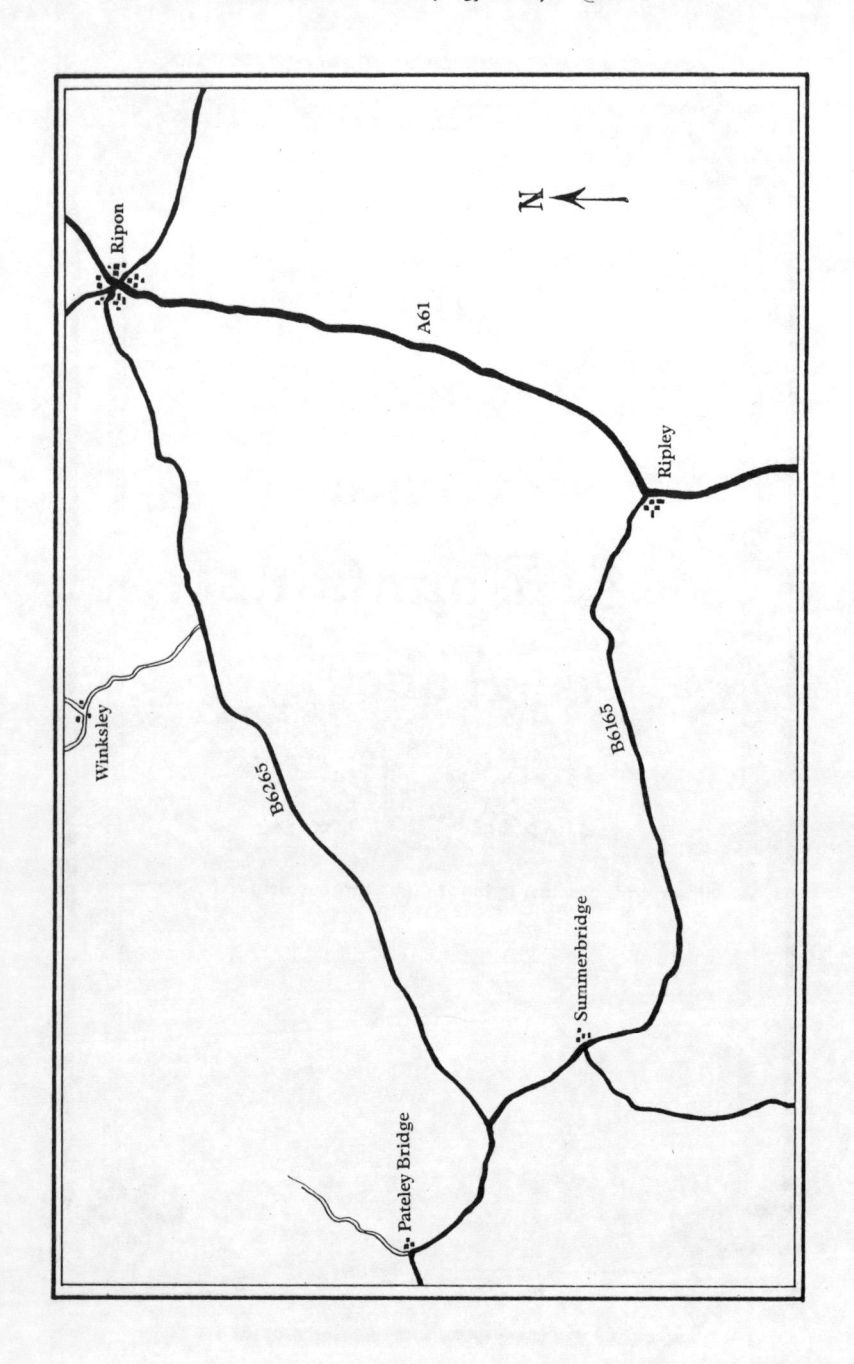

Ghost Trails of the Yorkshire Dales

A Super Centre

Pateley Bridge is a popular centre for exploring the eastern section of the Yorkshire Dales.

It was a medieval town of some importance with major routes to York and Ripon. There is a market charter dating from the 14th. century, but the once popular market has now been abandoned.

Pateley Bridge has an impressive setting with the main street rising steeply from the river. This little town has much to offer the visitor. There is a good range of hotel and guest house accommodation, a well-appointed riverside campsite, and a worthy range of shops. The Crown Hotel and the Coffee House offer excellent and inexpensive food. For gentle exercise the 'Panorama' and riverside walks are highly recommended.

The Nidderdale Folk Museum - based in the former (1863) workhouse - is one of the most imaginatively thought out small museums in the UK. This delightful folk collection offers considerable insights into life and tradition in the Dales.

The town also displays many visible links with history. There is the 17th. century sweet shop and apothecary's house on High Street. The writer, Rudyard Kipling, stayed at Hawkridge House on Wath Road where his godfather was a methodist minister. St. Cuthbert's Church houses a bell saved from nearby Fountains Abbey.

An Old Haunt

The Crown Hotel, which dates from 1750, was linked in its early days with a woman variously known as either Molly or Polly Menwith.

Molly was a flame haired 'working girl' whose Amazon-proportioned charms proved attractive to travelling gentlemen. In order to maintain herself, and an increasing tribe of children, Molly also kept a 'winter list' of local customers. Many of her 'young gentlemen' shared a common bond : Molly was as much part of their formative education as first lessons in practical poaching.

Despite commendable customer loyalty, the approach of middle age brought a downturn in trade. Molly made up for this loss of income by systematically blackmailing former clients.

But one late summer's day, her ample body was found in an eddy pool in the river. It was said that she had fallen from the slippery bank whilst intoxicated.

For two months rumours flew faster than summer swallows. Though it was known that Molly Menwith was partial to a drop of gin, she had never been known to slide from a vertical to horizontal position without first negotiating a fee. And not a penny piece was found on her.

But slowly the river of speculation dried to a trickle, and Molly became a winter memory to be placed alongside the chill of the first snowfall. The occasional visitor would make a polite enquiry, only to be told the tragic news of her demise.

A likely lad called Jake witnessed Molly's 'return.'

It was an evening in late January when he left The Crown and stumbled to a favoured spot in a nearby alley to answer the pressing call of nature.

As he stood within the cloud of steam, he became faintly aware of a large presence behind him. It was impossible to turn, but he immediately recognised the husky voice of the woman who made a ribald comment about the effect of cold weather.

Jake was confused. Perhaps the best part of a gallon of ale had clouded his memory.

" But I thought you were dead, " he said as he turned.

" But I am, " came the reply.

" Then what do you want? " he asked anxiously.

" Just what is owed me, " announced the spectre.

At this point the conversation ended. But the encounter had restored some sobriety and Jake ran like a rabbit.

The following day he told his trusted friends of the Molly Menwith comeback. They promised discretion, so within a few hours the whole town had the story.

There are rumours of several further encounters with the ghost of Molly Menwith. But, as it was suggested that the ghost only appeared to former clients, there was a natural reluctance perhaps to admit to a sighting. But for a time it was noted that even the sturdiest specimens of local manhood were unwilling to venture onto the moonlit streets alone.

A fund-raising effort for Molly's young family was begun by several influential gentlemen to ensure - in the best spirit of philanthropy - that they were well provided for. It may be coincidence, but it is said that the ghost made no further appearances once deeds of trust were signed and the youngsters happily settled in the home of a Bewerley curate.

The Big Wheel

The nearby Watermill Mill - now a rather pleasing hotel - was founded as a flax mill at the turn of the 19th. century. At the side of the building is what is probably the largest overshot wheel in the country.

The largest overshot wheel in the country

Ghostly Noises

After the mill closed the site was regarded with some superstition. Strange creaking and groaning noises were heard in the vicinity, but there seems to be no reports of a ghostly manifestation.

Take the B6165 towards Summerbridge. Turn sharp left at Summerbridge after the Old Bakehouse Restaurant. The road up Hartwith Bank is marked as unsuitable for heavy vehicles, and it is. A steep wooded lane leads to the top of the bank. Pass Helme Pasture Holiday Lodge (which sports the sign of a witch on a broomstick) and carry straight on at the crossroads. There is a large National Trust car park at Brimham Rocks.

The Bonny Rocks Of Brimham

The National Trust have done much to preserve the natural beauty of this splendid site. The well-stocked Tourist Information Centre is a good place to start. Outside the building there is a superb panoramic view, which in ideal conditions can extend for 36 miles. Points of interest include three power stations. The Drax station is nuclear fuelled.

The millstone grit outcrops were once regarded as the work of druids.

Brimham Rocks

This false impression is reinforced with names such as Druid's Altar and Druid's Head. It was even thought that the narrow tube-hole in one rock served as an oracle - with the 'Wise One' standing behind giving astrological predictions.

Many of the rocks received their titles from the Victorians, who obviously had fertile imaginations. Names such as Indian Turban and Dancing Bear also reflect some of the popular preoccupations of the era.

The natural drama of this rocky backdrop has been exploited regularly by television, and perhaps most successfully in the filming of Margaret Taylor Bradford's 'A Woman of Substance.'

Brimham Rocks

The Stuff Of Legend

It is said that eloping lovers called Edwin and Julia were pursued by the irate girl's father. He caught them at the top of a crag, but they leapt into space and landed safely.

Concerned perhaps by the possibility of an action replay, the father forgave them immediately. The crag where this is said to have occurred is still called Lover's Rock.

The Third Man On The Crag

Brimham Rocks had always been popular with climbers. In August 1977 Matt Latham and Denis Evans of Leeds were enjoying an afternoon's sport when disaster struck.

Denis explains : " We weren't doing anything very tricky, " but it was a blazing hot day. I knew I was in trouble when I started to feel groggy.

" Matt was 30 feet below. It was free climbing, so we weren't roped up. I pushed my body tight against the rock. I was swaying now. I tried to call down for help but the words stuck in my throat. There were flashing lights in front of my eyes. I could feel the pulse in my neck throbbing. I was trying desperately to hold on. Then I felt strong hands round my wrists and I was being pulled upwards. Suddenly I was on my knees but safe at the top of the crag. I looked up at the shape of a very tall man standing over me. All I can remember is a bushy beard and something very odd. He had bare feet.

" My head was spinning. I lay down on the rock and closed my eyes. Everything was spinning. I think I blacked out for a few seconds. The next thing I remember is someone calling my name. It was Matt. "

Matt takes up the story. " I'm ashamed to say that I hadn't noticed Denis had a problem. But when I got to the top he was lying there alone on flat rock.

" I couldn't get him down on my own, but we'd seen some people climbing on an adjacent crag. I started to scramble down the easy way. But help was already on the way. A club climber had seen the rescue and had gone for reinforcements.

" Later there were lots of questions about the third man on the crag. How did he manage to vanish so fast? Why didn't he stay around to help? Where did he suddenly appear from in the first place?

" Climbers are a fraternity. You'd expect someone to come up with a name, but not this time. But we heard the story of the phantom climber.

Brimham Rocks

" It seems that one of the greats - Conor O'Brian - practised here from time to time before the First World War. He was a tall man, and immensely strong. And, he had the habit of climbing whenever possible in bare feet. He claimed this was much better than wearing boots because you could feel into each tiny crevice with the toes. Conor was a real adventurer of the old kind - a professional sailor who years later made a voyage round the world in a small boat. But I don't know what happened to him after that.

" He'd come to grief here some time in 1912 or 1913. Nothing serious - just cuts and bruises. But he was immensely grateful to those who helped. He said he'd like to return to repay the debt. But with the war and all, I don't think he ever did.

" But a kind of folklore built up after a Danish climber got tangled in his own rope and was helped out by a tall man in bare feet. It was treated as a bit of a joke at first. There's not much in the way of mountains in Denmark.

"The story was repeated. There were more rescues and the helper always disappeared straight afterwards. This earned him the nickname 'The Lone Ranger.'

" But the bare feet were also mentioned a couple of times. To be honest, that's the only link to Conor O'Brian, so maybe that's wishful thinking. But I'm sure of two things. There was no human being on that crag when Denis and I started climbing, and there was nobody there when I reached the top. I've thought a lot about it since. I don't believe in ghosts, but I can't come up with a better explanation."

Return to the crossroads, then turn left for Burnt Yates. Pass Well House of the left.

Hot From The Coven

Well House is associated with a 17th. century coven.

The story is that two local women, Meg Collingham and Margaret Taylor, held a contest to see who was truly ' Mistress of the Black Arts.' The winner was to become undisputed leader of the coven.

The well-attended meeting was held in a barn above Well House. Both women impressed their followers with amazing acts of depravity, bloody sacrifice, and fearsome curses. But just as it seemed that the contest was heading for a draw, Meg produced her trump card.

This was a special distillation, which 'when combined with fire, gave forth an aroma that would incite the passion of any man.'

As the coven rules forbade the presence of 'any man, saving the Devil himself,' a substitute had to be found. Meg had planned her strategy carefully, and was therefore less surprised than most to find Roger the ram tethered conveniently nearby.

But Roger was less than pleased to be led so close to the fire. Just as the potion was to be sprinkled, he broke free and charged for the open doorway. As Meg poured her flammable phial, Roger left a stream of toppled witches in his wake. Searing flames and a rampaging Roger now combined to cause consternation.

The thatch caught as first Roger, then the witches, fled the barn. A few hours later there was little left but embers.

At a rather less eventful meeting some weeks later, Margaret Taylor was declared Queen of the Coven.

Turn left onto the B6165 and head towards Ripley.

The Virginia Creeper-covered Bay Horse Inn at Burnt Yates is a pleasant pit-stop.

The inn features a foul-mouthed phantom.

A Honeymoon Haunting

It seems that a former landlord's wife had a voice and lungs to combat the spaciousness of the main bar. Even sotto voce her words were easily overheard. Most of them were derogatory to her husband, which did little for his self-esteem.

Her comments became more colourful as the years went by. Indeed there can have been few inhabitants of the area who did not know the supposed detail of the husband's failings as both landlord and lover.

The poor man seemed to bear all this with uncommon good humour. But, when his wife added insult to injury by declaring an intimate association with several of the regulars, he could stand it no more.

One fine morning two large men in white coats entered the premises carrying a straight-jacket and muzzle. Despite her vociferous appeals nobody lifted a hand to help as she was dragged away.

There were nodding heads throughout the district when it became known that the landlord's wife had been committed to an asylum. It is said that her screams were stifled by socks for several months, before she gave up the unequal challenge and expired.

There were few who were surprised when the landlord announced his intention to marry the seductive (but softly-spoken) barmaid.

A large and happy crowd attended the wedding ceremony and the beer flowed freely through the evening. At midnight the last guest departed and the newlyweds made their way to bed.

But the fire was burning low, so the landlord rushed down the stairs once more to fill the scuttle.

The new bride removed the warming-pan from the fresh linen and undressed quickly. She was about to leap into bed when she felt the firm grip of a hand on her shoulder. She spun round, expecting to meet the embrace of a husband - distracted perhaps from his declared purpose of fuelling the fire.

But only the shadow of her own reflection stared back from the dressing table mirror.

This fearful moment was almost forgotten as the landlord entered the room and purposefully bolted the door. Indeed they were joyfully snuggled beneath the sheets before there was any further indication of an unwelcome presence.

The a hideous, but familiar ring of laughter, dampened their passions faster than a bucket of ice-water. The young bride screamed softly, then clung to her husband as they hid beneath the sheets.

There was one more ghostly guffaw, then silence. And that was it. No more noise, no further manifestation. These strange phenomena were enough to ruin a wedding night, but happily not a marriage.

Indeed, some say the vile voice was heard for the last time that night. Others suggest that the trumpet tones can still heard from time to time, especially on winter evenings when the rivalry of ladies darts is renewed...

Turn right at the major traffic island for Ripley

The French Connection

Ripley has a distinctly French feel. It was modelled on an estate village in the Alsace by one of the more eccentric members of the Ingleby family in the 1820's.

Marston Moor

Cromwell stayed here on the eve of Marston Moor in July 1644. Although the battle was a decisive defeat for Prince Rupert, the parliamentary forces failed to follow up their victory.

Family Fortunes

Ripley has been associated with the Ingleby family since 1320.

The attractive 16th. century castle remains a family home. Indeed, a modern Ingleby wrote the excellent guide book.

The hour long tour is heartily recommended. The guides seem hand-picked for their enthusiasm and natural rapport with the public. An amazing gift shop sells an imaginative range of gifts and souvenirs. These include quality publications, fancy goods and smoked beer.

The splendid grounds and lake have much to do with the vision of Lancelot 'Capability' Brown. The building contains fine period furniture and paintings. Of special interest is the priest-hole discovered in 1964 within the panelled walls of the Knight's Chamber.

Ripley Castle

The Smell Of Gunpowder

Guy Fawkes spent many happy teenage days here before soldiering in the Spanish Netherlands.

He is remembered as one of the conspirators who were caught with barrels of gunpowder beneath the Houses of Parliament on the night of November 4th./5th. 1605.

The sustained enthusiasm for Bonfire Night in these parts may have something to do with a natural Yorkshire suspicion of Westminster.

The Polite Phantom

The ghostly figure of a nun is said to knock at doors in the castle, but it does not enter the room unless invited.

The Curse

One former member of the Ingleby family was in the Casanova league. He kept a number of mistresses scattered around the county to ensure that even the most arduous travels were not unrewarded. His favourite mistress was hidden at Padside - a hamlet between Blubberhouses and Pateley Bridge.

The longsuffering Ingleby wife became increasingly annoyed by these infidelities. Finally she tracked down the Padside mistress and paid her at visit. At the end of this fiery encounter, both mistress and philanderer were roundly cursed. Wished upon them was a most unpleasant end, and an extended 'sentence' of haunting.

Within the year the first part of the curse was fulfilled. He was riding with the hunt when he became all but decapitated by a sturdy, and unfortunately low branch of a tree. Less melodramatically, she succumbed to a cold that turned to pneumonia.

The Haunting

For many years after these events the wraiths of a 'gentleman and lady companion' were regularly seen walking in the Padside area.

Victorian ghost-hunter, Alfred Dunn, described the phenomenon : 'This was a wonder of which I had heard much. After waiting for three nights at the appointed place I was inured to disappointment.

'It was the week after the full moon. The mist hid the ghyll (a wooded ravine) and thus I did not at first discern them. First, they were but wraiths in the gloaming, but by and by they drew close.

He bore the manner of a gentleman, but she I declare was not of such degree.

'He took her arm as they crossed by the footbridge below. I was not a chain (approximately 20 metres) from them. They whispered as lovers, but were oddly discomforted. By and by the lady wept. At last they turned again to the ghyll. I followed privily 'til these misfortuned shades were consumed by the mist.'

Rising From The Ruins

The original parish church at Ripley was built rather too close to the stream, but it is believed that stones from the original building were used to construct the present building in the early 15th. century.

Architecturally the church is perpendicular and decorated. It contains memorials to the Ingleby family - most notably the tombs of Sir Thomas who died in 1369, and Sir William who died in 1617. The churchyard features an unusual Weeping Cross, and stocks are sited below the Village Cross.

Return to the traffic island and take the A61 to Ripon

Underrated Ripon

Ripon is not top of the tourist itinerary, partly perhaps because of the more obvious attractions of York and Durham. But those who do take time to explore these lovely old streets will find much to surprise and delight them.

The Wakeman

The market square is a good place to begin. The black and white (13th, century) Wakeman's House is set to the right as you face the Town Hall.

The Wakeman's horn has been traditionally blown at 9 pm at the market cross, the same time as the curfew is sung in the minster tower. In the 1920's the corporation agreed to a second sounding of the horn outside the Mayor's (Wakeman's) house.

A white-clad figure has been seen from time to time at an upper window in the house. This is said to be the ghost of the city's most famous Wakeman, Hugh Ripley, who in 1604 became Ripon's first Lord Mayor.

The Precious family, who lived in the house for almost century from 1820, were often woken by footsteps and moving chairs. The white-clad apparition in the front bedroom was regarded as an additional member of the family.

The Wakeman was a city official charged with the task of warning the populace of impending peril. At one time this job entailed much more than the largely symbolic blowing of the horn. It was a responsible position that included a regular review of the city defences. The Town Hall inscription sums up the difficulty of the job: 'Except ye Lord keep ye City ye Wakeman waketh in vain.'

The list of Wakemen reveals that the longest incumbent of the post was John Simmons

The Town Hall, Ripon

(1848 -88), and the shortest tenure (one month) was that of John Lonsdale in 1968.

The Cathedral

The magnificent cathedral provides reason enough for a visit to Ripon.

Bede described how a small monastery was founded 'in the heathen town of Ripon' around AD 655. Both the monastery and its church were destroyed by Viking raiders in the 9th. century. This, and similar attacks elsewhere, all but eliminated Christianity in Yorkshire.

Only the Saxon crypt - now the splendid treasury - remains of St. Wilfred's 7th. century building. This was created under the high altar of the church, and was used as a chapel until the Reformation. A narrow hole in the north side is called St. Wilfred's Needle. Linked perhaps to the medieval practice of Trial by Ordeal, it is said that the ability to crawl from the crypt to the adjoining passage is a sure sign of chastity. It is a sign of the times perhaps that the climb has been rarely attempted in recent years.

Ripon Cathedral

The cathedral contains many other points of interest. Particularly notable is the choir screen (1480) and the exquisite carving of animal subjects on the misericords. The bishop's throne features an elegant elephant.

Leave the square and pass the cathedral to find the ancient foundation of the hospital and chapel of St. Mary Magdalen.

The Hospital Ghost

Ripon also features the noteworthy remains of two medieval hospitals - St. Anne (the Maison Dieu) and St. Mary Magdalen.

Founded by Archbishop Thurston of York in the early 12th. century, St. Mary Magdalen was a facility devoted to lepers and blind priests.

A youthful spectre has been seen crossing the road here on several occasions. The ghost is said to be that of a schoolboy who was run down by a cart. It is also said that the ghost has been seen wandering around the precincts of the solitary chapel.

Local resident, Michaela Todd, describes her encounter in 1973.

" I was on my way home from school. It was late November and the street lights were just coming on. It was the clothes that made me notice him. Short trousers and a black fustian jacket, with just a flash of white collar underneath. And he was tiny. The jacket swamped him.

" He seemed sort of lost. He stood on the kerb as if to cross. There was nothing coming, but he turned away and carried on along the pavement.

" It wasn't far from where I lived then, but I'd never seen him before. You get to know people. Not their names maybe, but you fix them with times and places.

" I tried to catch up with him. He looked round once and started running. I stopped. He looked round again and he stopped. It was as if he was playing a game. As soon as I started walking again, so did he. Then he stopped again. He seemed to bend down and pick something up from the pavement. I was quite close now.

" He was still looking at whatever it was in his hand when he stepped into the road. I thought he'd seen the car coming. You couldn't miss it. It was a great big thing with bright twin headlamps. I don't know if I called out before the car hit him. But the odd thing was there was no sound.

" And the car just kept going. I couldn't believe it. I rushed into the road myself. The horn was loud. I don't think the second car missed me by very much, The driver shook his fist at me as he drove past.

" I just stood on the pavement and stared. There was nothing in the road except the white line. I looked around. I couldn't see him anywhere.

" By the time I got home I was shaking. My mum knew something was wrong. She made me tell her, but she didn't say anything at first. She talked to Dad about it later. They told me it was my imagination.

" I'm married and have children of my own now, but I still get the nightmares. Sometimes I just close my eyes and I can see it all again - every detail. I don't like going to that place. Something really horrible happened there a long long time ago. "

Law And Disorder

Before leaving Ripon a visit to the Police and Prison Museum on St. Mary's Gate is recommended. The building was once a house of correction, before becoming a police station. The arresting exhibition - housed in the former cell block - charts the history of law and occasional disorder in the city since the Norman Conquest.

The Friendly Festival

Ripon has become known as one of the friendliest and safest cities in the UK.

This is a comment regularly made by visitors who come to enjoy the traditional Festival Week which is held annually during the third week in August.

At one time the city wives used to rise at four in the morning to make pastries of jam and curd, or apple and cheese. This were left outside front doors for visitors to enjoy. A more secret Ripon recipe is for Wilfra tarts, which are baked to commemorate the return of the saint from exile.

The festival today is more cultural than culinary, but it is no less enjoyable for that. Some of the events are booked up well in advance, so it is well worth checking ticket availability.

Take the B6265 to Fountains Abbey.

Fabulous Fountains

Even the approach to Fountains Abbey gives more than a hint that it is something

Fountains Abbey

special. How many private roads have white lines and roundabouts?

Millions of visitors make the site a major operation of logistics and conservation. Fortunately the National Trust provides plenty of parking and a most alluring visitor centre.

The abbey is simply the most famous and largest ruined abbey in Britain. The first view through the trees of the majestic towers is breathtaking.

The same Archbishop Thurston who established St. Mary Magdalen at Ripon, later helped to diffuse a dispute at the Benedictine House of St. Mary's at York. The result was that 13 monks were taken into Thurston's protection in 1132, and two months later made their way three miles up the River Skell to land he had given them.

Fountains Abbey

The site was deemed most suitable and Thurston himself confirmed the election of Prior Richard as the first abbot.

One problem was that the community was too small to survive, so the brothers turned to the French Cistercians - known as the farmer monks - for recruitment. The result was an abbey of exceptional efficiency that it became even wealthier than the mother house at Citeaux.

The 'white monks' sustained a pretty rigorous order. No underwear was permitted. The habit of undyed wool was worn with woollen or cloth stockings and leather boots. Breeches were provided only for travelling, after which they were washed and returned to the common stock. The diet was more subsistence than substantial and attention to devotions was maintained throughout the coldest of weather.

Lay brothers were regarded as second division monks. They were often illiterate, but thus avoided the worst excesses of austerity in return for their labour. The bonus of being a lay brother has been summed up as 'less church, more sleep, and more food.'

Accommodation was based on a similar apartheid system. In addition to separate dormitories, the lay brothers had their own infirmary and refectory. Most bizarre of all was the way they were separated from the 'choir monks' by screens in the church. They even took communion at a separate altar.

A combination of bad luck, bad harvests, and bad management brought a decline during the 14th. century. Nevertheless the abbey survived Black Death and Scots Raids only to fall victim to Henry VIII's dissolution in the 16th. century. The last Abbot, Marmaduke Bradley, served as a king's commissioner. His reward for such devotion to duty was a pay-off pension of £100 a year. The prior received £8, and the monks £6 each - roughly equivalent to the pay packet of a country priest.

King Henry sold the grounds to Sir Richard Gresham. The more accessible stone was used to build Fountains Hall.

Perhaps the best way to see the abbey is floodlit on a summer's night. The careful selection of the floodlights somehow enhances the scale. and plainsong adds to an atmosphere that is often enough to chill the bravado of the most exhibitionist youngster.

It is rumoured that plainsong is heard from time to time in winter too. But as there is nowhere in the UK that captures the mood of the past quite as well as Fountains Abbey, it is perhaps a most likely spot to encourage the mind to play tricks.

There are legends of Friar Tuck, a ghostly guide, and the wandering Blue Lady of Fountains Hall. But all this is best left off the page. For in this special place the visitor will know that every stone has a tale to tell.

Fountains Abbey

Return along the B6265 to Pateley Bridge

Ghost Trails of the Yorkshire Dales

No. 4 Gargrave, Skipton & Wharfedale

This circular motoring tour takes approximately eight hours

Ghost Trails of the Yorkshire Dales

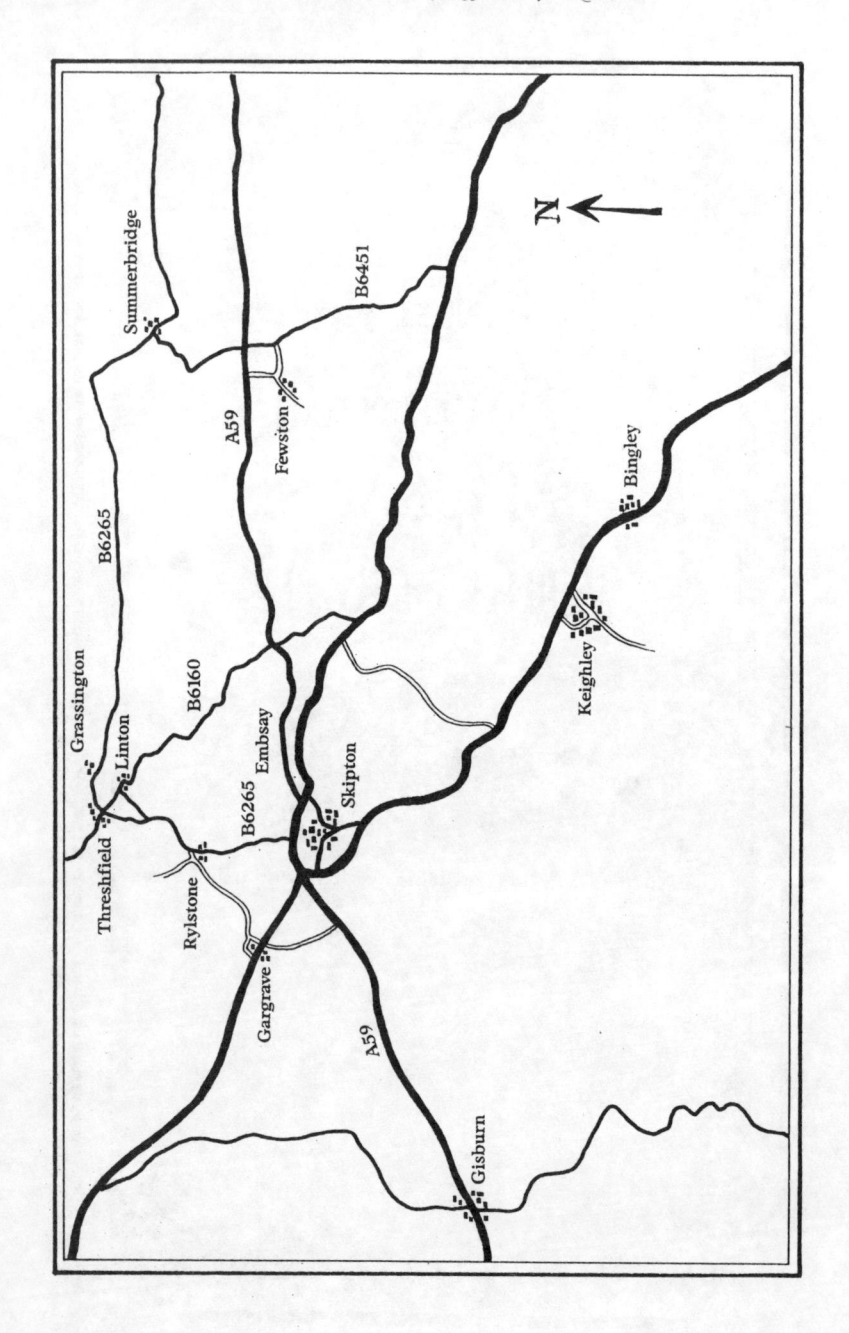

Pennine People

Gargrave is favourite resting place for Pennine Way walkers.

The village is rather more spread out than most grey stone villages in the Dales, which gives Gargrave a unique character. The needs of the long-distance walker are admirably met by local guest houses, hostelries and cafes. The 'stately modern' Eshton Hall, and 17th. century Friars Hall are also of interest to visitors.

A Famous Phantom

Gargrave's most famous phantom was that of Tiny Thwaite, a 16th. century blacksmith.

Tiny was built like the proverbial brick outhouse, and is reputed to have stood two metres tall in specially made boots. If true, it is not surprising that it is said he was as almost as fearful to behold in life as in death.

Tiny was a Orkney islander, whose original surname - Twatt - was probably taken from village of his birth. How the name came to be changed is less certain. It may be a natural derivative, but it is more entertainingly argued that this could be the mark of Thomas Bowdler, the late 18th. and early 19th. century doctor and publisher, who sanitised everything from Shakespeare to folk tales.

The story begins with Tiny 'Thwaite' leaving his island home after committing the foulest of murders. Escape to England meant he could avoid the jurisdiction of Scottish law.

Tiny had the most terrible of tempers, and was best not approached during a bout of drinking. The love of his life was a publican's wife, whose general approach to fidelity was not to be discovered in a compromising situation with more than one man at once.

It may be because of the uncertainty of this relationship that Tiny acquired the unnerving habit of punching both animate and inanimate objects. For the animate this lead to deep resentment. For the inanimate it meant replacement rather than repair.

It is said that the good people of Gargrave knew a human time-bomb when they saw one and resolved to remedy the situation.

The publican drew the short straw. A heady brew was prepared for the blacksmith in a special barrel that was sealed only after the addition of digitalis. But the dose - 'enough to kill a pack of dogs'- was just sufficient to cause the giant some painful stomach cramps. Perhaps he suspected the landlord's intentions. The next day the unfortunate man's body was found with the 'neck broken like that of a chicken.' His grieving widow left Gargrave a few weeks later with a regimental recruiting sergeant.

No further attempts were made on Tiny's life. He was heartbroken and no more than the shell of his former self. Less than a year later he succumbed to an 'apoplexy' (possibly a stroke) and was found lying face downwards by the roadside.

It is said that no hand was raised to rescue or revive him, and the chill of the winter's night left him as stiff and still as a statue. He was buried in unconsecrated ground.

For more than a century his ghost terrorised the village and surrounding countryside. This fearsome phantom was particularly active in the hours before dawn, and would knock so violently on doors that 'the very bones of the building would shake.' Slumbrous householders were raised from their beds to face the stark choice of greeting the ghost, or calling for the carpenter.

An exorcism was carried out in 1671. This seemed to do the trick as there are no records of further manifestations. But it is noted that even today the front doors in Gargrave are generally of the sturdier kind.

The Unreaped Harvest

The lovely parish church can be found across the bridge on the minor road to Broughton.

A granite cross in the south-east corner of the parish churchyard marks the last resting place of Iain Macleod who died in 1970. This 'most able politician of his generation' became Chancellor of the Exchequer for the last three weeks of his life.

Take the minor road to Broughton

Broughton is a 'blink and miss it' hamlet close to the A59. It contains some fine farm buildings, with external steps to the upper stories.

Nancy And The Evil Eye

During the 16th. century a Broughton man was sure that a spell had been cast upon him. Local opinion offered two likely perpetrators - the witch Nancy Newgill, and a tinker noted for 'the evil eye.'

The remedy was put a counter-spell on both of them. The problem with this was the theory that the spell on the innocent party could 'rebound.'

The man decided to accuse both candidates first, and to judge their reaction. Nancy Newgill used fearful oaths in her declaration of innocence, but the shifty-eyed tinker gave a less convincing performance. He was therefore targeted for the counter-spell.

A 'wise man' was enlisted to make a rough cast of the figure. Then a mixture of boar's lard and bullock's blood were daubed onto the clay. The contents of the mould were then divided. Part was put in water, rolled into a ball and thrown away. The rest was burnt and the ashes were buried in the churchyard.

The man felt better by the evening. The tinker went blind,

Turn westwards to East Marton on the A65. Behind the Cross keys Inn a narrow lane drops to Abbot's harbor.

A Hidden Gem

Abbot's Harbor is a little gem only discovered by the most discerning of travellers, or those who walk this canal section of the Pennine Way.

The hamlet features an 11th. century building - now an excellent restaurant. This was once part of a Cistercian farm settlement, on the route between Fountains and Salley Abbeys.

Tiny slippers can be found in a crevice in the restaurant wall. Local superstition has it that these are an effective remedy against evil spirits.

The nautical theme of the restaurant is most obvious in a sign that once had its home in a famous waterside inn. The rubric reads 'Miss Dolly Camp can accommodate six seamen a night.

Abbot's Harbor

Continue along the A65 to Gisburn

Over The Border

The four mile diversion into Lancashire's Ribblesdale is well worth it.

Gisburn is often dismissed by travellers as a staging post between Clitheroe and Skipton. But those who take the trouble to explore more thoroughly will be rewarded by some interesting finds.

A Saxon cross and Norman tower greet visitors to the large parish church. Snow Hill is one of many outstanding old buildings, and the Ribblesdale Arms is one of the oldest surviving inns in Lancashire.

The ancient parish church, Gisburn

How To Get Ahead

This historic hotel dates from 1635. The building and interior were both designed by Thomas Lister - a man of unusual artistic tastes. At one time walls were adorned with portraits of noblemen with one thing in common. Each had spent his final moments resting his neck on the axeman's block.

The Phantom Of Room 13

The visitor to Room 13 will still encounter a bed with shroud-like foot carvings. It is said that a lustful Lord Ribblesdale seduced a young girl in this room.

The ruins of Salley Abbey (at Sawley near Gisburn)

In the fulness of time Lord Ribblesdale was laid to rest in a silver coffin. The vengeful spirit of his victim however sleeps less easily. A tearful but revenge-minded ghost is said to make a regular return. Consequently the room is never let to ordinary guests. The ghosthunter however may just be granted special dispensation. A bell is hidden behind the bed in case the human resident requires assistance.

Return along the A65 to Skipton

Situated on the Airedale Moors, Skipton (once Sheeptown) is perhaps the most delightful market town in Yorkshire. The town has a special charm that seems to grow with each visit, and the inhabitants rank amongst the most cheerful and welcoming in Britain.

Important Landmarks

Skipton is dominated by its 11th. century castle and 12th. century church.

A Place In History

The original timber church fell into disrepair around the end of the 11th. century, and the foundations of the stone structure were laid at the beginning of the 12th. Much of the finance for the venture was raised by the Canons of Bolton Priory.

The Parish Church of the Holy Trinity has many interesting features. There is a lovely 16th. century oak roof that was greatly repaired following a lightning strike in June 1853. One of the roof bosses - surmounting the third nave arch from the tower - is a 'Green Man' - complete with oak branches sticking out of his mouth. The tradition of the Green Man is almost certainly pre-Christian. Much like the Easter Egg, associations are with birth and renewal.

The 14th. century tower was damaged by stray cannonballs during the Civil War, but again it was the 1853 lightning strike that brought down a pinnacle that weighed one and a half tons.

A medieval fresco near the font represents the Hand of Death. One function of the Church was to keep the populace in line. Frescos such as this served as a useful reminder of man's brief tenure on earth and the judgement that would follow.

The church also contains several Clifford family memorials. The most moving, but least noticed, is the small memorial placed here by Henry the last Earl of Cumberland. It is to the memory of his three sons who died in childhood. A translation of the Latin reads: 'On this small memorial Henry, the father, bewails with much grief Francis, Charles and Henry. AD 1631.'

Holy Trinity Parish Church, Skipton

The Castle And The Cliffords

The rocky outcrop on which the magnificent castle stands had a palisaded fortress as early as 1090. But the constant threat of Scots raids persuaded the de Romaille (or de Rumilly) family to build in stone. The gatehouse arch and towers are part of this early structure.

But it is the fighting Cliffords who will be forever most associated with the fortunes of Skipton and her castle.

Robert de Clifford was granted the castle by Edward II in 1310. Robert had proved his resourcefulness in many battles with the Welsh, and the king saw him as an insurance policy against further incursions from north of the border. Robert was killed at Bannockburn in 1314.

The castle we see today was shaped by generations of Cliffords through the next four centuries. During this time the fourth Lord fought at Crecy (1314), the sixth died in Germany, and the seventh was killed at Meaux in France where he was leading a siege force for Henry V.

The Cliffords carried their banner on the losing side through much of the Wars of the Roses. Thomas Clifford was killed at St. Albans in 1455.

His son, John was called 'The Butcher' because of his slaughter of Yorkists at Wakefield (1460). He is also remembered for personally removing the head of the Duke of York and hanging it on a spike over the gates of the city. It is believed that he was also responsible for the murder of the Duke of York's young son.

John Clifford was killed in equally brutal circumstances at Towton the following year.

Family fortunes were restored by the most colourful Clifford of all - Henry the tenth Lord. [featured in Chapter 2.] Henry was almost 60 when he held a major command at Flodden in 1513.

By the mid 17th. century urgent repair and restoration work was required. Much of this was carried out by Lady Anne Clifford. A yew tree planted in the small but lovely inner courtyard in 1659 is a reminder of this remarkable lady.

Tradition has it that the ghost of Lady Anne rides in a spectral coach towards the castle gates whenever the death of the Lord of honour is imminent. But as no record seems to exist of a single sighting, this is probably best described as a delightful piece of folklore.

The castle is a must for the visitor. It is one of the most splendidly preserved in the UK and captures many moods of the past.

JMW Turner visited Skipton in 1816 as part of his painting tour of the Dales. A legacy of the visit are several fine sketches done around Mill Bridge which show the castle perched resplendently on its crag. The thousands who look at the same scene through their viewfinders each year may not realise just how little it has changed in almost two centuries.

Skipton Castle

When Midnight Strikes

For the ghost trailer much of the interest is focused on the Great Hall. A fine figurehead, though fixed firmly to the wall, is said to come alive at midnight.

The Phantom Guard

And another fearful encounter is possible at Skipton Castle.

It is said that a strange and lonely vigil has been observed, most frequently from below. Peter Corrigan of Keithley encountered the phantom guard in 1987. He tells the story like this:

The phantom figurehead, Skipton Castle

" I was walking under the castle walls when something made me look upwards. What I saw was so weird it stopped me dead in my tracks.

" He was a tall man. There was some armour - I remember a breastplate and helmet - and I think he wore leather leggings. At first I thought it was a show, but as I watched I knew it wasn't that. Something was wrong. At first I wasn't sure, but then I realised it was the legs. They weren't really moving, but he was. He was almost floating along. It was a bit like one of those half-animated cartoon characters.

" The face was odd too. I can't say there was no face - it was more no features. Well, there was something there, but it was somehow unfinished. I can only explain it as a black and white sketch in the middle of a colour picture.

" No I wasn't scared. Later maybe, but not then. What was there to be scared of? I think I knew it was a ghost, but somehow he seemed to have a right to be there.

" I don't know how long I was watching. Maybe a minute or two. But suddenly it was all over. He was there and then he wasn't. There was no fade out. He just vanished."

The Mandeville Connection

The history of this haunting may just be found in the 12th. century.

The story begins with the divorce of King John from his first wife, Avice (otherwise Avise or Hadwisa) of Gloucester during the first year of his reign. Naturally he kept her dowry, but this rankled greatly with her second husband - Geoffrey de Mandeville.

The Magna Carta gave Geoffrey at least a partial revenge. It also taught him much about flexible allegiances and coercion. During a whirlwind career he extorted valuable charters from both Stephen and Matilda, as well as honours such as the Earldom of Essex.

But then it all went horribly wrong. In 1142 he was caught in another round of intrigue with Matilda and forced to maintain himself as a rebel and outlaw.

In the summer of the following year he came to Skipton to seek support from his friend, de Romaille. As the visit was 'unofficial', trusted guards at the castle were instructed to be more vigilant and silent than ever.

It seems that one of these men, an officer called Thomas Meltham, had a regular 'arrangement' with one of the ladies of the town. It was to her he revealed the name of the illustrious guest at the castle.

The rumour circulated quickly, and Geoffrey de Mandeville was forced to flee with his 'merry men' back to the relative safety of the fens. Meanwhile, de Romaille tracked the source of the leak and plugged it. Thomas Meltham was thrown into the castle's deepest dungeon.

De Mandeville's Robin Hood existence ended with a disembowelling sword thrust two years later. It is said that Thomas Meltham survived for more than 40 years, but never again saw the light of day. Could this be why the unfortunate phantom only seems to make an appearance during daylight and in the very best of weather?

The Leeds-Liverpool canal, at Skipton

Hob House

Just outside Skipton is Hob House - the once supposed home of a particularly hideous hob.

But by all accounts the hob was willing to please. Turning up in the fields one day he offered to help with the threshing of the corn.

Whilst the workers welcomed the assistance, they found the proximity of the hunchbacked, halitosis-toothed, wart-encrusted creature too much to bear.

The hob was given a red hood to cover the worst of his ugliness. This offended his sensitivities, and he wandered off never to be seen again.

Take the B6265 towards Grassington

The village of Rylstone once enjoyed spectral visits from a highwayman. But nothing much seems to be known about this character and the manifestations ended some time before the First World War.

The White Doe Of Rylstone

The remains of Norton Tower can be located a mile to the south of the village.

This was once the home of Francis Norton, one of the few local worthies who did not join the Pilgrimage of Grace in 1536. This was the backlash against Henry VIII's decision to dissolve the monasteries.

The following year Francis was invited to join the Rising of the North - an attempt to restore Catholicism led by the Earls of Northumberland and Westmorland. Again he had no stomach for it.

However, nine other members of the Norton family were involved in insurrection. For their efforts they were arrested and imprisoned at Barnard Castle. Two of them later kept an appointment with the axeman at York.

The condemned men were Thomas and Christopher Norton, Francis's younger brothers. It was this that spurred Francis into a single act of defiance. He took a banner from one of the king's supporters. For his crime he was hunted, caught and murdered by Sir George Bowes and his henchmen. The site of the murder - a field close to Bolton Priory - was at least convenient. Francis Norton had already left instructions that he was to be buried there.

Other members of the family now felt that England was not an entirely safe place for the Nortons. Only young Emily - 'as fine a lass as ye may know' - decided to remain behind.

One of Emily's childhood companions was a young white doe. The creature followed her everywhere until reaching maturity. Then it was released into the park herd to do what a doe has to do.

Following her isolation, and the confiscation of the property, Emily hid with friends, wandered the hills, and made regular visits to the family graves at Bolton Priory.

On one of her solitary rambles Emily met the herd on the hills. The White Doe left the gathering and ran to join her friend. Wordsworth penned a typically understated account of the encounter which begins :

> 'She melted into tears -
> A flood of tears that flowed apace
> Upon the happy creature's face.'

The doe joined Emily on her constant round of rambles and prayers at the priory. But the unhappiness of this existence affected Emily badly. She aged prematurely, and soon became a few pence short of a pound in the faculties department. Perhaps this contributed to her early demise, for all too soon the unfortunate Emily was laid to rest alongside her mother at Rylstone.

The doe dutifully spent the rest of her days commuting between the Norton graves at Bolton and Rylstone.

Leave the B6265 after Cracoe, and take the signposted minor road to Linton-in-Craven

Lovely Linton

Linton-in-Craven is arguably the most attractive village in the Yorkshire Dales. Cottages nestle around the well-kept green. There is little to break the silence other than birdsong and a gurgling of the stream.

The only ugly object in Linton is a mini-basilica set at the edge of the green. This commemorates the 1949 News Chronicle award for the 'loveliest village in the north.'

The prosperity of Linton is due in no small measure to the Fountaine family. Their influence is most obviously marked by six

Lovely Linton

18th. century almshouses and the hospital chapel which was founded in 1721.

The Fountaine Inn retains the mood of the past, but it is also splendidly airy and comfortable. The visitor will be delighted to find one of the most thoughtful and varied menus in Yorkshire.

The writer, Halliwell Sutcliffe, lived at White Abbey - a magificent property that is no more than an Olympic stone throw from the heart of the village. The odd thing about the house is that the external dimensions do not correlate to the available space within. The suggestion is that White Abbey contains perhaps a priest hole, or a hidden passages.

The Headless Horseman

Linton may offer the occasional glimpse of a rare breed of phantom - the headless horseman.

Victorian ghost-hunter, Alfred Dunn, noted his appearances as 'most regular', but did not supply further details. As this manifestation does not seem to have been witnessed within living memory, it is likely that the even the most determined ghost-trailer will be disappointed.

But the background story is so bizarre it is worth re-telling.

It is said that a royalist messenger was dispatched from Skipton with a document for sympathisers in Linton. Unfortunately he ran into a Cromwellian patrol near Cracoe and literally lost his head in the skirmish that followed.

But rather than let the document fall into the hands of the enemy, the messenger managed to continue with the mission. He fell from his horse almost at the feet of a local curate as he rode into Linton. Although obviously unable to speak, his last act was to hand over the message.

Some say the nature of the haunting suggests that the curate was of the Parliamentary persuasion, and so each ghostly ride is a fresh attempt to place the paper in the right hands. If that is the case, the lack of sightings in recent years may indicate that the headless horseman was ultimately successful in his quest.

Cross the B6160 and follow the road downhill to the riverside. The car park is half way between the parish church and the falls.

Days Of The Dragon

There is much symbolism in the name and sighting of the ancient parish church.

This was almost certainly a pre-Christian site of worship. The church, in common with many dedicated to St. Michael, is sited on low ground at a bend in the river. The saint is associated with the Jewish battle against 'heathenism', and a river bend is often linked to the pre-christian dragon cult.

Earliest worshippers here may have included Norsemen, but the physical evidence is inconclusive. What exists today is a building that dates from the middle of the 12th. century.

Sacrilege

The church's most famous relic - the Linton Crucifix - was made in brass perhaps a century before the Norman Conquest. It was found near a local ford in 1835. A picture can be found in the south arcade. The crucifix itself was stolen in 1980.

Also stolen was an ancient sundial from the churchyard. It was replaced with a replica, but this too was taken. Today only the stone base remains.

What does remain are several interesting headstones. West of the church one stone records the demise of a woman 'whose mysterious maladie, which baffled the skills of medicine, was a curse that deprived her of taking any food or drink for nine weeks.'

On the south side there is the grave of John and Henry Davies who were lead miners from Grassington. John is remembered as having 'one of the deepest and most extensive bass voices in the kingdom.' Henry 'was alike celebrated for his clear, melodious tenor voice.'

Phantom Feet?

A riverside path leads to the falls. It is a short but pleasing walk.

From time to time people enjoying the riverside wander have been alarmed by the sound of heavy footsteps behind them. This has variously been described as 'several' or 'many' walkers. But a soon as the wanderer turns around, the sound disappears. There is no sight associated with the sound, nor has any reasonable explanation been given.

Return towards Linton, but turn right along the B6160 to Threshfield.

An unusual tale is told in Threshfield. It is one of those stories that is so improbable it is just about possible to believe it.

The Phantom Fiddler

They say a female fiddler, Pam, once lived at Threshfield School.

She had a mischievous nature and liked to play 'games' at night.

Once, the rector left a sermon on his desk. Pam pretended he was an intruder and beat him around the head when he returned in the dark to collect it.

Pam's taste for high spirits was often focused on the bottle. On one occasion she became so drunk that the frantic fiddle playing became unbearable to the rector's ears. He burst into the room. An argument turned to a fight, and the rector's strong hands closed rather too tightly on her throat.

Then, according to the story, he buried her in the playground.

But this was not the end. Pam's ghost (or some say hob) returned to torment him. Naturally, the main instrument of torture was the fiddle. Indeed, the phantom fiddling finally drove him out of his mind.

Sanctuary

The Well of Our Lady has long been regarded as a sanctuary against the powers of darkness.

A local legend tells of a man on the way home from his favourite hostelry when he was chased by imps. He ran to the sanctuary of the well. They surrounded him but were unable to come too close. At the first light of dawn they were forced to depart.

Veteran ghost-trailers will have noted the frequency of attacks by fairies, imps, and demons in the Yorkshire Dales. Oddly, the victim is always male, and the attack invariably occurs just after pub closing time.

Follow the B6265 to Grassington. Cross the Wharfe Bridge and pass the village centre. Plenty of parking is available close to the National Park Information Centre.

Town Or Village?

Grassington was once the Saxon settlement of Girston. It is usually referred to as a dales village, but qualified as a town when granted a fair and market charter as long ago as 1282.

Fun At The Fair

The fairs were major social events. The round of frivolity included chasing pigs with soap-soaked tails, archery contests, sword dancing, bull and badger baiting, and the customary round of excessive eating and drinking.

The fair ended in 1860 : a victim of countryside depopulation and improved communications to Skipton and beyond.

The National Park Centre

The excellent National Park Centre in Grassington reflects the growing importance of the village as a tourist centre. There is information available on a wide range of Dales activities.

A popular rose-tinted view of the Yorkshire Dales is that the area is some kind of magical wilderness. But there is little that has not been shaped in some measure by man.

The National Park do much to heighten a balanced awareness of the area. It belongs first to the people who live here, and the emphasis is therefore more on seemly than cosmetic.

Grassington provides many excellent examples of the way the appropriate balance has been maintained.

The Women's Revenge

Men found guilty of beating their wives in Grassington were subjected to the ordeal of steng-riding. The man was forced to balance uncomfortably on a long pole which was carried through the streets. The custom was for the townswomen to greet him with a torrent of rubbish and verbal abuse. If it is true 'that no man ever took a second ride on the steng,' then the deterrent effect of public humiliation speaks for itself.

The Grassington Send-off

Funerals is Grassington were also very special events. A stand of chairs and tables was created for the coffin to be displayed outside the home of the deceased.

Hymns were sung in the street before a slow procession made its way to St. Michael's Church at Linton.

Lead Mining And The Upper Wharfedale Museum

Lead mining was the mainstay of the local economy until the middle of the 19th. century. The industry developed mainly through the investment of the Duke of Devonshire.

Many of the buildings are Georgian, which reflects the 'boom years' of mining activity. There is a cluster of mining cottages around the market place, two of which have been developed as the Upper Wharfedale Museum. Here you can discover original fireplaces, a beehive oven, fine oak beams, and a splendid collection of farming, mining and household equipment.

There are claims that the ghost of a miner has been spotted in the Springfield Road area. Unhappily, enquiries have uncovered no further details.

The Old Hall

13th. century Grassington Old Hall is one of the oldest domestic buildings in the north of England.

Nowt For Warmth But Her Petticoat

The actress Harriet Mellon developed her art at the local theatre cottage. It was once said 'she had nowt for warth but her petticoat' - a phrase not so much indicative of poverty as humble origins.

Harriet joined the famous Edmund Kean's players in London, but her career on the boards was relatively brief. Not for the first time in history, a young actress caught the eye of a wealthy man - in this case the banker, Thomas Coutts. In later years, as Duchess of St. Albans, it is said that Harriet had a wardrobe full of silk and lace petticoats.

The Grassington Barguest

The Grassington Barguest was featured in a newspaper report in 1881.

The story is that a likely lad called William enjoyed 'a few beers' with friends before walking home along a lonely track by Rylstone Fell. He thought he heard a rattle of chains, and felt a chill breeze as something seemed to pass him.

After hearing the chains a second time, he started to run until he reached a small wooden bridge. As every Dalesman knows - the beastly barguest is supposedly afflicted with an inability to cross water.

As William climbed the hill path towards Linton he thought he heard the sound again, but there was still no sign of the beast. But as he reached home, loud brushing and clanking noises announced the presence. Indeed, there it was lying on his doorstep in all its loveliness. William described it as a huge hairy sheep.

Naturally he was not keen to approach it, even though this specimen was clearly the runt of the barguest litter. But the only way into the cottage was through that door, and the way was blocked by a somnolent and snoring barguest.

He summoned up courage and roused the creature with a well aimed kick. Lazily it opened it's saucer-sized eyes ; three of them

(he said) - red, white, and blue. He kicked the beast again, and set about it with a stick. Still it refused to budge.

His shouts woke his wife who ran downstairs to the scene of the commotion. As the door was opened the creature rose and moved off, first slowly, then at best barguest pace.

William later suggested the barguest knew that the odds were stacked against it : 'For that missis o' mine 'as a terrible temper,' he said.

The Price Of Adventure

On Sunday 14th. July 1967, a group of ten cavers set out to explore the three miles of underground passages at nearby Mossdale Caverns.

The morning drizzle turned to heavy rain while they were underground. Four cavers emerged late in the afternoon, but the rest were trapped underground as the system flooded. The entrance remained submerged until the following day when at last a rescue could be attempted. Four bodies were found almost immediately, and the fifth a few days later. It was judged dangerous, if not impossible, to remove them. The coroner therefore approved a plan to allow the bodies to be sealed in the cave. Some time later caving colleagues of the deceased interred the remains in a high-level chamber at the end of the system.

The Blacksmith's Crime

There is an unusual plaque outside the main street smithy. This commemorates a celebrated crime.

Tom Lee lead a busy life. He was a skilled blacksmith, landlord of the notorious Blue Anchor Inn, and a part-time burglar. He had a fiery temper and sturdy physique which meant that most people were not inclined to cross him.

One night Tom, dressed as a highwayman, waited in the shadows of Moor Lane. His target was the 'running postman' - a one man 18th. century Securicor operation, carrying wages for the lead miners.

Tom leapt onto the postman and clubbed him to the ground. But this large Yorkshire lad was not prepared to give up so easily.

After landing a couple of good punches, the 'postman' reached for his pistol and shot Tom Lee in the arm.

Tom retreated into the darkness and hid. Later he staggered to the house of Dr. Petty, who dressed the wound. The doctor agreed not to tell the authorities. Oddly, this seemed to have more to do with patient confidentiality than fear of the hot-headed blacksmith. Dr. Petty even warned Tom Lee about his future conduct.

Some time later the doctor visited the Angler's Arms at Kilnsey. Here he found Tom Lee in a heated argument with local farmer, Dick Linton. It was clear that Linton was accusing Lee of various crimes which the blacksmith denied. When the argument looked likely to end in fisticuffs the doctor intervened by gently reminding the blacksmith of their little secret.

Later the same day Tom Lee waited behind a wall by a lonely lane. As the doctor returned from his rounds, the blacksmith pulled him from his horse, kicked him to the ground and slashed at him with a knife. When Dr. Petty moved no more, the blacksmith dragged the body behind the wall and ran back towards the village. His intention was to catch the unfortunate doctor's horse before an alarm was raised.

An hour later Tom Lee arrived home, weary and splattered with blood. He confessed his crime to his wife and persuaded her to help him bury the body. The matter was now urgent because Tom had failed to catch up with the horse.

Also living in the house was a young apprentice called Bowness. The blacksmith and his wife soon realised that their raised voices may have been overheard. They went to the apprentice's room and found the lad cowering on the bed.

They gave him two choices. Either he could become an accomplice, or he could join the doctor in a peaty grave.

The three of them waited for nightfall, then went to recover the doctor's body. At first it seemed to have disappeared, but soft groans from some way off in the darkness told their own story.

As they approached the spot the doctor cried out for help. Tom Lee battered the last of the life out of him with a stick. Then the three of them rolled the corpse in sacking and buried it in the peat bog.

Early the next day the riderless horse was found and the search began. Tom Lee joined one of the search parties, but this public-spirited effort only helped to fan the flames of rumour. But nothing was found.

Some weeks later the apprentice, Bowness, left for a job in Durham.

This could have been an end of it, but Tom Lee made a fatal mistake. He overheard a group of Blue Anchor regulars talking about the way peat preserves corpses.

He returned to the burial place with his wife and dug up the doctor. Then they hid the corpse under bundles of hay and drove the cart towards a suitably deep pool in the Wharfe. But as the body slid into the water, the action was observed by a sharp-eyed young man on his way home from an evening's courting.

The doctor's body was recovered by the authorities and Tom Lee was charged with murder. Twice he was freed for lack of evidence, largely because his wife could not give evidence against him.

For the next three years Tom Lee was condemned only in the eyes of those who had few doubts that he had committed the crime. But when a young Durham blacksmith cleared his conscience by telling of his own part in events, it was clear that the law would soon settle with Tom Lee.

He was sentenced in York, and a large crowd turned out for what was to be a memorable hanging. Tom Lee mounted the platform fearlessly, thanked the Lord for the warmth of the July day, and asked the hangman to tie the knot securely.

The body swayed in a gentle breeze for more than an hour before being cut down and returned to Grassington. Here for public gratification the corpse was hung from a tree at Grass Wood.

The spot became something of a tourist attraction, and Grassington entrepreneurs enjoyed the 'I knew Tom Lee' bonanza for several years. Indeed it was only when interest declined that the pitiful remains of the blacksmith were removed and buried on Gibbet Hill.

The Screaming Skull

Grass Wood, where the corpse of murderer Tom Lee was displayed, is on the delightful Wharfedale Tourist Trail. But it may be that this is not such a pleasant spot at night.

In July 1952 Joe Mason, and girlfriend Angela Marsden, were enjoying a walk in the evening air when they heard a sound that stopped them in their tracks.

Joe takes up the story : " It wasn't quite a scream. It was more of a high pitched moan - not loud, but constant.

" I looked around but there was nothing. But then I did hear a scream. It was Angela. She was pointing ahead. I still couldn't see anything. I think she tried to say something but I'm not sure.

" Then I saw it myself - the skull. It seemed to be hanging in the air above us. It wasn't far away. It wasn't attached to anything. It was rocking from side to side. The jaw was open, but the noise seemed to be coming from all around it.

" I thought it was calling to us. It sounds stupid now but I don't remember feeling frightened. We just stood there looking up and listening to that strange sound.

" After a while Angela tugged at my arm. I said something daft like 'I want to watch for bit longer,' but she was on her way. I followed, but then I turned round. It was still there, but it seemed closer to the ground.

" It was strange, but there was no chance of trickery. We were in an open spot. It's just one of those things. You don't believe in something like that' til you see it. But I won't mind much if I never see anything so spooky again."

Return to Cracoe on the B6265, then take the minor road to Gargrave.

Ghost Trails of the Yorkshire Dales

No. 5
Kirkby Stephen, Swaledale & Tan Hill

This circular motoring tour takes approximately six hours

Ghost Trails of the Yorkshire Dales

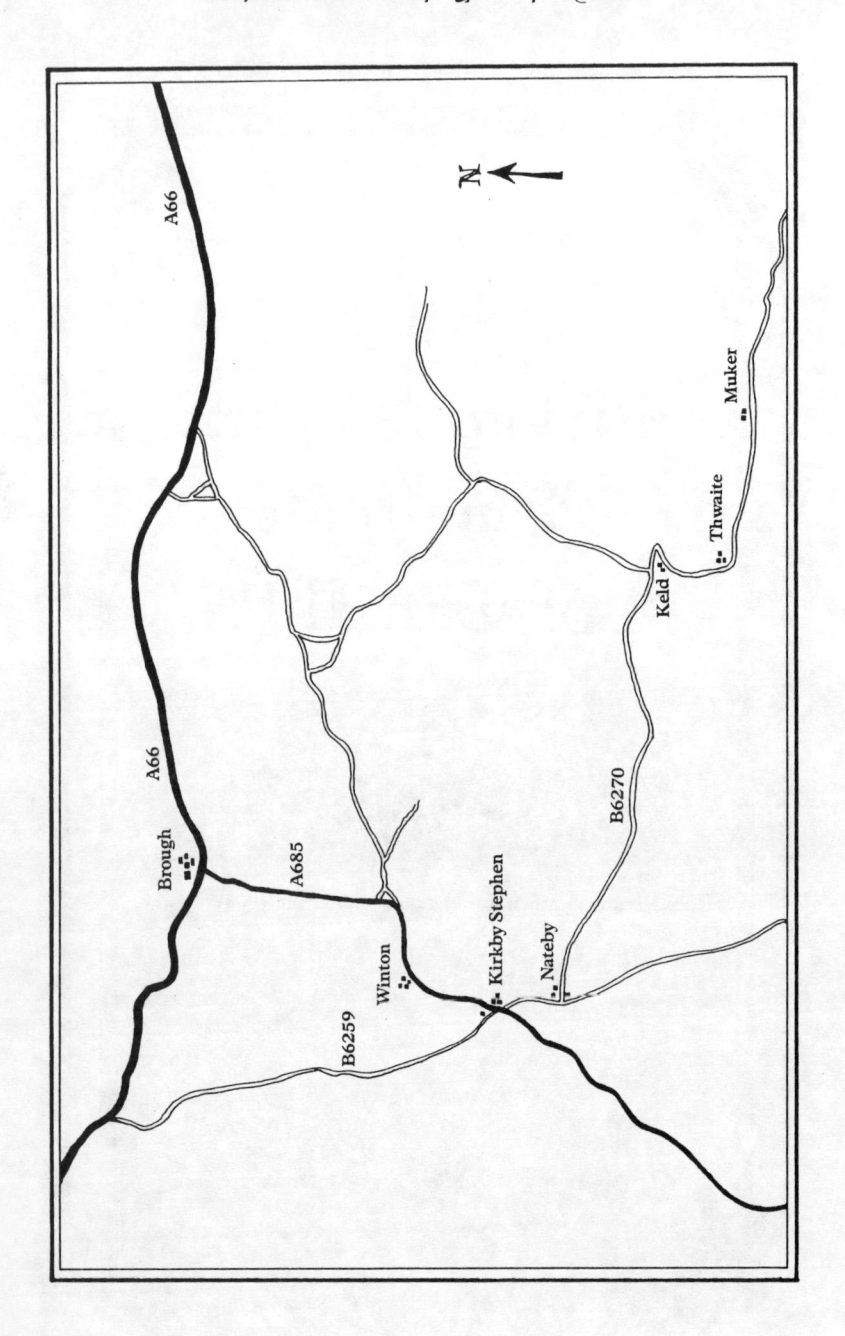

Begin at Kirkby Stephen

The Wild West

Kirkby Stephen is all too often ignored by visitors to the region. In part this is explained by its fringe position and, even by Dales standards, isolation.

This small town is surrounded by some of the least hospitable terrain in the UK. To the west is Ravenstonedale and 'wild' West Fell - a delight during the few weeks that pass for summer. To the north-east is Stainmore - a desolate spot where the curtains were drawn on the Kingdom of Northumbria in AD 954. To the south is Wild Boar fell, once perhaps the last wilderness in England, and the Mallerstang Valley which contains the slight remains of Pendragon Castle - said to be the fortress of Uther Pendragon, King Arthur's father.

All this has shaped Kirkby Stephen. It is a sturdy grey place that echoes the wilds that surround it.

The Butcher's Wife

One of the finest old buildings is now owned by Penrith Farmers Estate Agents. It is a former butcher's shop which features a 17th. century gallery.

A local tradition has it that a former butcher's wife revenged herself on an unfaithful husband by taking a meat cleaver to him. She escaped punishment for the crime by claiming he had deserted her. By the time the authorities heard whispers of something more sinister, the last pie had been sold and eaten.

She maintained to her dying day that the errant husband took naught but his woolly coat and departed. However, a suspicion remains that he is perhaps more likely that he left the shop wrapped in a muslin bag and flaky pastry.

An Unseen Hand

Less than a century ago there were reports of poltergeist activity at a house now numbered 89 High Street.

Plates and ornaments went into self-destruct mode, and clocks in the house regularly stopped at a quarter to midnight. Even more oddly it seems that an assortment of objects - from keys to candles - would disappear only to turn up a few days later. An exorcism was carried out, and a contemporary account claimed 'these ministrations stilled the unseen hand.'

Temperance Time

For several generations there was an enthusiasm amongst Dales folk for 'signing the pledge against the demon alcohol.' This was largely to do with Methodism - a major influence during the 19th. century.

Kirkby Stephen retains one of its Temperance Inns.

Bull Baiting

The Temperance Hotel, Kirkby Stephen

This 'innocent and pleasurable pastime' was officially banned in 1835. The practise was to test the bravery of dogs by setting them on the bull. Much money changed hands on the outcome. The dogs were specially bred for the 'sport' with great power in the forward part of their bodies and jaws. The bulldog and larger bull mastiff can be traced back to these times.

Things did not always go according to plan. This 1783 account from a small northern town makes sobering reading.

'The bull was that enraged that he three two tradesmen, one of whom had his leg broken and the other received a severe wound in the head. Another bull broke loose and galloped wildly through the streets tossing dogs lifeless in the air and trampling those who blocked his way. The market was crowed with men an women. They were clustered in the windows, on the cross, the town hall stairs, and in the shambles.'

A Game Of Taggy

In local folklore those out after eight o'clock in the evening were likely prey for the demon Taggy. As a warning to all the Taggy Bell was traditionally rung from the parish church at the evening curfew.

Of course there were those who would brave the wrath of the demon if the 'rewards' seemed to be worth it. Courting couples were once said to 'be shirkin' Taggy' and regulars at the public houses had to 'hie from Taggy'. Both expressions died out from popular usage around the turn of the 20th. century.

Confusing and contradictory accounts do little to establish any meaningful form or impression of Taggy. The word was used up to the 17th. century to indicate a troll-like boggart whose preferred diet was peat-roasted human flesh. By the 18th. century however it had come to suggest a more ethereal demon that dealt mischief to those it caught wandering after dark.

Fear has long been the European way of instilling discipline and obedience in young people. One of the simple joys of parenthood is to pass on the nightmares of youth to the next generation. 'Taggy' is probably little more than the Kirkby Stephen version of a thorn almost universally sown into the garden of the young mind.

The Last Wild Boar

Sir Richard Musgrave is credited with killing the last wild boar. His tomb, which was opened many years after his death, contained a well preserved tusk.

An Evil That Lived On

The ghost of a nobleman has been spotted at various points along what is now the A685.

The spectre is said to be that of the evil Lord Wharton, former Lord of the Manor and President of the Peculiar Court of Ravenstonedale.

Lord Wharton was in fact very much a law unto himself. He committed terrible crimes against his tenants, and reserved particularly unpleasant penalties for wrong-doers. Torture was invariably followed by a painful lingering death.

In the local popularity stakes Lord Wharton was placed slightly ahead of the Black Death, but well behind most other forms of pestilence. As an old man he was struck blind whilst riding home. This affliction was commonly believed to be divine retribution.

The ghost is said to be a pathetic spectacle. The well-dressed, but mud-soaked nobleman is seen at the roadside. Sometimes it is said his own frail fingers grasp at the forehead, and the palms of his withered hands cover the eyes. But the memory of Dales folk is elephantine. Nobody pauses to offer solace or assistance, for it is said that the first kind word will forever end the ghostly torment.

A Kind Of Revenge

Kirkby Stephen Parish Church contains the tomb of Sir Andrew de Harcla (otherwise Harclay or Hartley). Sir Andrew was a local hero.

The reign of King Edward II was a turbulent time in English history. The balance of power between baronial alliances and the King seemed always to balance on the razor's edge.

The king's treatment of favourites was perhaps the greatest bone of contention. One of these, Piers Gaveston, had won control of lavish grants and had twice been forced into exile by the barons.

Each time the king encouraged his return. Finally, certain barons decided that his downfall should be guaranteed permanent. In June 1312 he was lynched on the orders of Thomas, Duke of Lancaster.

For a short time the situation improved, but the game began again when new favourites were installed. This time it was the Dispenser family who caught the royal eye. They were most notably represented by the two Hughs - father and son.

Again the barons grew increasingly annoyed with the growing influence of these royal favourites. They were particularly indignant about the favours heaped on Hugh Dispenser (the son), who like Piers Gaveston before him had become the personal favourite of the homosexual king.

A collision force of feeling lead to an insurrection. This ended with victory for the king at Boroughbridge in 1322.

The role of Andrew de Harcla in events leading up to the battle was crucial. The baronial force, lead by Thomas Duke of Lancaster, had to cross the Ure to make good their retreat to the border. Here they encountered the thin ranks of de Harcla's Cumbrian levies who held the position just long enough for the pursuing royalist force to encircle the barons and force their surrender.

But Sir Andrew became rapidly disillusioned. He was soon trapped in political intrigue, and when the Dispensers dealt their cards against him, his fate was assured. But given his previous allegiance, the severity of the sentence sent shock waves through the country. This great warrior suffered the 'crusader's death' - he was hanged, drawn and quartered. The remains were returned to Kirkby Stephen and a brass plaque in the church marks his burial place.

When King Edward II met an even more hideous end four years later, this was perhaps judged locally as no more than he deserved.

Having brutally stamped out insurrection, Edward fell foul of the enemy within - his wife Isabella. This ultimately led him to become the most famous royal murder victim in English history.

First Edward was forced to give up the crown, then he was transferred from Kenilworth to Berkeley Castle.

Here, in the words of the chronicler : 'Every indignity was inflicted on him. He was systematically ill-treated in the hope that he would die of disease. When his strong constitution seemed likely to prevail over the ill-treatment of his enemies, he was put to death by means of a red-hot wire thrust through the lower orifice into his entrails by way of a horn tube.'

It was announced that the deposed monarch had died a natural death. He was buried in St. Peter's Abbey at Gloucester.

Hartleys, Musgraves And Whartons

This fine old building also contains some notable Musgrave tombs, including that of 'Wild Boar' Richard.

This has been a place of worship for more than 11 centuries, although the present building dates from around 1220.

The Hartley Chapel denotes the importance of this family in local history. The name is derived from de Harcla.

The Wharton Chapel contains the tombs and effigies of Thomas - the first Lord Wharton - and his two wives. The Whartons have been major local benefactors and indeed it was the first lord who founded the grammar school in 1566. The fourth Lord, Philip, began the distribution of bibles to children - a tradition that continues to this day.

Bread And Holy Water

The church also contains unusual 18th. century bread shelves. These were once stacked with loaves for the poor. There is also a fine 17th. century font.

A Viking God

Perhaps the most notable relic to be found in the church is the 10th. century Loki Stone. This is a carved Anglo-Danish cross shaft which features a hirsute chained devil said to represent Loki - a Viking god. This pre-conquest symbol of the devil in human form is one of only two known to exist in Europe.

Kirkby Stephen Parish Church

Take the B6270 to Nateby, then over the high moor to Keld

Beauty And The Bleak

The journey over the high moor and down the Birkdale Beck is one of the most dramatic in the Dales. To the west Wild Boar Fell rises above Mallerstang Common. To the south there are the slopes of Great Shunner Fell.

Birkdale Beck begins as a trickle which builds to a torrent after it is joined by Whitsundale Beck above Keld. There are impressive water falls and a landscape that has been called 'Beauty and the Bleak' (though on this approach to Swaledale the reverse applies).

The Birkdale Beck

The Price Of Lead

Keld is a collection of hamlets based on the former mining industry. The decline in these parts dates from the 1880's, by which time foreign competition had seriously eroded the market.

The Kinnaird report (1862/4) suggests that the average lifespan of a Swaledale miner was 46 years. The biggest killers were consumption (at least in part induced by the climate) and bellan - a form of lead poisoning.

It is not known when mining activity began, but certainly many of the skills had been developed before the Roman occupation.

The Swaledale orefield included Arkengarthdale and the northern side of Wensleydale. One area of intense activity was Gunnerside - once dubbed the Klondyke of Swaledale.

The metal - for which men women and children toiled in mines and smelt mills - was used for such diverse buildings as French cathedrals, German castles, and even the Tower of London.

The industry developed alongside the growth of the monasteries in the 12th. and 13th. centuries. Later owners, such as the London Lead Company, bankrolled Dales mining from Elizabethan times onwards.

Ore was first taken from bell-pits - shallow shafts with galleries running from the base. Later came the adits which were horizontal shafts cut into the hillside.

The ore was revealed by a process called hushing. Here water was trapped in temporary dams, then released to expose the rock. Repeated hushings have left gashes of up to 100 feet deep.

The area around Keld today is very much an open air museum of the industry. The most obvious 'exhibits' are the scars on the landscape, but a little patient exploration will reveal much more. Areas around the old shafts and workings can be hazardous and should not be approached too closely.

A safer option may be a visit to the Swaledale Folk Museum at Reeth. Here carefully selected exhibits and thoughtful displays admirably chart the history of the Dales lead miner.

Ghost Trails of the Yorkshire Dales

Unearthly Intervention

On a warm August day in 1924, Charles Mannion, a retired Richmond schoolmaster, set out to explore a adit shaft above Keld. His diary records such detail as the lunch he ate on the hillside, and the way a kestrel took a small creature from a grassy knoll no more than 200 yards from where he was seated.

In the same matter-of-fact tone the entry continues: 'It was not straightforward to gain entrance. All was greatly overgrown and some attempt had been made to create a blockage, but soon all was circumvented and I was able to light my lamp.

'From within I heard a curious noise. I considered at first this to be windrush, and continued. Again I heard the noise and now recognised human articulation. I was bemused and enquired if I could be of service.

'This curious articulation was repeated, and now I recognised within it my own name and the word 'withdraw.' I turned in some trepidation for the ingress. As I stood without I gave much attention to the report of debris falling behind me. Had I remained within the

A waterfall above Thwaite

adit there is small doubt of my demise.

'I related my encounter to Mr. Kearton. His observation was that my life was spared by unearthly intervention, and it was by no means the first occasion of similar circumstances.'

Follow the B6270 down to Thwaite and Muker

Thwaite and Muker are both worth this diversion from the circular tour. The villages are remarkably different in character from each other. They represent just two of the many faces of Swaledale.

Just Cause Or Impediment

Thwaite's old chapel closed in the early 1980's. It has been converted into two holiday cottages.

A chapel wedding in 1895 became the focus of a simmering row. When the questions of 'just impediment' were put, representatives of both families gave a number of 'reasons' why the marriage should not proceed. These 'reasons' amounted to little more than slanders based on real or imagined wrong-doings. This reflected more than 50 years of inter-family feuding.

Once the minister had assured himself that there was no legal reason why the marriage should not be solemnised, he cleared the chapel of 'all but those necessary to make a wedding'. As the service continued ill-feeling turned to fisticuffs in the street. The happy couple emerged to be greeted by a vision of blood-splattered Sunday suits and broken noses.

Two wedding breakfasts were held - one at Thwaite, and one at Muker. Happily, the newlyweds were not separated for long. They left the feuding behind and opened a successful business at Barnard Castle. The popular account suggests that neither of them ever visited Swaledale again.

This is an appropriate, but sadly inaccurate, end to the story.

They did return - if only once - for a more conventional family wedding some five years later.

A Phantom Feline?

Thwaite was once said to feature a phantom feline. This was a large black cat that would be found sitting outside the cottages of inhabitants about to make a debut in a better world. The cat was said to have continued with these warnings of a imminent visit from the Grim Reaper for more than a century.

This jewel of folklore, in common with many of its kind, is probably based on a number of grimalkin generations. In the Yorkshire Dales much the same principle can often be applied to the more extreme claims for human longevity. In almost every case father and son shared the same name and a remote dwelling.

Picture Pioneers

Thwaite was the birthplace of Richard and Cherry Kearton - pioneers of wildlife photography. A subscription plaque for Richard Kearton, who died in 1928, can be found in Muker. This recalls his work as a naturalist, author, and lecturer.

Also In The Picture

Muker is rightly popular with Dales visitors. Although the size of the habitation limits facilities, there is adequate provisioning and an excellent pub.

The Parish Church of St. Mary has pictures of incumbents from 1929 onwards. These reflect not only the changing trends of clerical dress, but also something of the character of the each incumbent. Peter Midwood, shepherd of this Swaledale flock in the 1990's, is pictured on his tricycle.

The Crackpot Witches

A family bible proved the unlikely source for a story of witchcraft set in the middle of the 16th. century.

The leader of the so-called Muker witches lived at Crackpot Hall, a mile to the east of Keld. The woman's name was Jane Yelland (or Yealand).

The coven met at a number of houses in Muker, but would observe the most significant dates of the black calendar 'by water, at Kizdown (probably Kisdon) force.'

Jane Yelland was supposedly skilled in hydromancy. This is divination by the movement of water. The method used was to drop molten lead into a pool and to make predictions according to the formations. Lammas Day was considered particularly portentous for an accurate oracle.

On August 1st. 1552 Jane foretold the death of the king 'afore next Lammas'. As King Edward VI was just 14 years old this was a surprising prediction. The whisper went out locally that Jane Yelland had staked the wealth of her witching reputation on a sure loser.

The young king died of tuberculosis on 16th. July 1553.

This tragic event enhanced Jane's standing, but caused sparks to fly from the anvil of jealousy. In time this put the authorities in a difficult position. Jane Yelland was a woman of some substance, and it had been previously possible to turn a blind eye to her dabblings in the black arts. But the fulfilment of the prediction raised the possibility of a spell cast on the monarch himself, and this could not be ignored.

It is said that Jane fled from Swaledale before the authorities could arrest her. But there were also whispers that she was being sheltered by one or another member of the coven.

Early in November 1553 the body of a woman was taken from the river near Healaugh. The corpse had been in the water for some time, so identification was difficult. But clues provided by clothing and jewellery were enough to convince valley folk that Jane Yelland had met a watery fate.

The body was burnt and the ashes scattered at a site only identified only as 'where ye waters enjoin.'

Return to Keld, and turn right to Tan Hill. The direction sign also indicates no caravans. The first S-bends of the bank are challenging to any motorist, and in poor weather conditions the road is best avoided altogether.

The Highest Hostelry

There are bleak moors in the Yorkshire Dales, but none are quite so desolate as Stonesdale and Stainmore. Tan Hill sits on a summit between the two. At 1732 feet it is the highest pub in the UK.

Each year hundreds of Pennine Way walkers escape the wind and rain for a medicinal dose of cheer and charm of this very special hostelry. Three foot thick walls, and the most famous double glazing in Britain, ensure the welcome is warm at any time of the year.

It is an accident of history that such a place should exist at all.

This has much to do with the route favoured by cattle drovers before the coming of the railway.

For most of the first half of the 20th. century the pub was run by the legendary Susan Peacock. Her fame was based on 'good country cooking' - a tradition that remains alive and well at Tan Hill today.

Her ghost, they say, makes an occasional appearance just to make sure that standards are maintained.

The Tan Hill Bogles

Visitors are always warned of the Tan Hill Bogle. Campers in particular are advised not to wander out alone during the hours of darkness.

The highest hostelry, Tan Hill

Tan Hill, it seems, has been home to a species of bogle for centuries, and regrettably attacks do occur. The pub staff will tell you that the bogles are notoriously acquisitive, so it is best not to leave food or valuables lying around, and all tent flaps should be carefully fastened.

A leaflet warns : 'If a member of your party goes missing, please report it immediately. (Although if the bogle has taken them it is unlikely that they will be found as the bogle-hole has never been discovered). We hope that your stay will be a pleasant one.

A prayer, penned by I. 'Bomber' Wilson, is offered as solace for the long dark night.

Nah Ah lig me damn to sleep
Ah pray The Lord mi soul to keep.
Should t'bogle come an't' bogle tek
Ah pray Ah'm deead afore Ah wek.
Amen.

Eric's Kingdom

The once proud Kingdom of Northumbria, that once stretched from the border to the Humber, came to an end at a lonely spot on Stainmore.

The stump of the Rey (from the Norse word meaning 'boundary') cross may have been commissioned by sympathisers of the Northumbrian cause. If this is the case, it is a unique and mournful monument. (The cross is now difficult to access because it stands on the wrong side of a duelled section of the A66.)

Eric Bloodaxe was a fearful figure, and a man capable of great savagery. At one point in his career he suffered exile and went pirating. His return was welcomed, not because of his popularity, but because he represented order and strong leadership. The alternative was to be ruled from the south - a thought no more palatable in the tenth century than it is today.

Little is known about the fateful Battle of Stainmore, but the courage of the Norsemen is clear enough. One scanty account refers to Eric's 'treacherous betrayal' and another briefly describes the bloody encounter like this : 'A dreadful battle ensued in which many English fell. But for every one that fell, three came out of the country behind. When evening came the loss of men turned against the Norsemen and many were killed.'

Turn west, and follow the road by Kaber Fell. Continue to take left forks until you join the A685 two miles north of Kirkby Stephen.

No. 6 Dent, Lunesdale & Ribblesdale

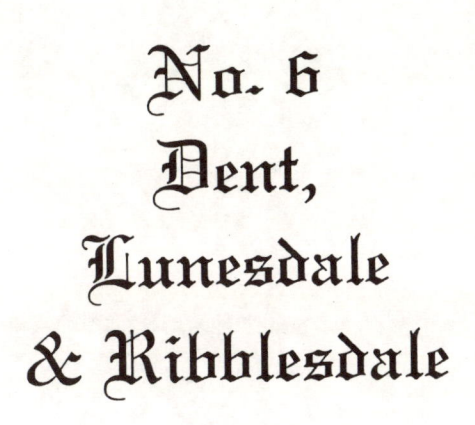

This circular motoring tour takes approximately ten hours

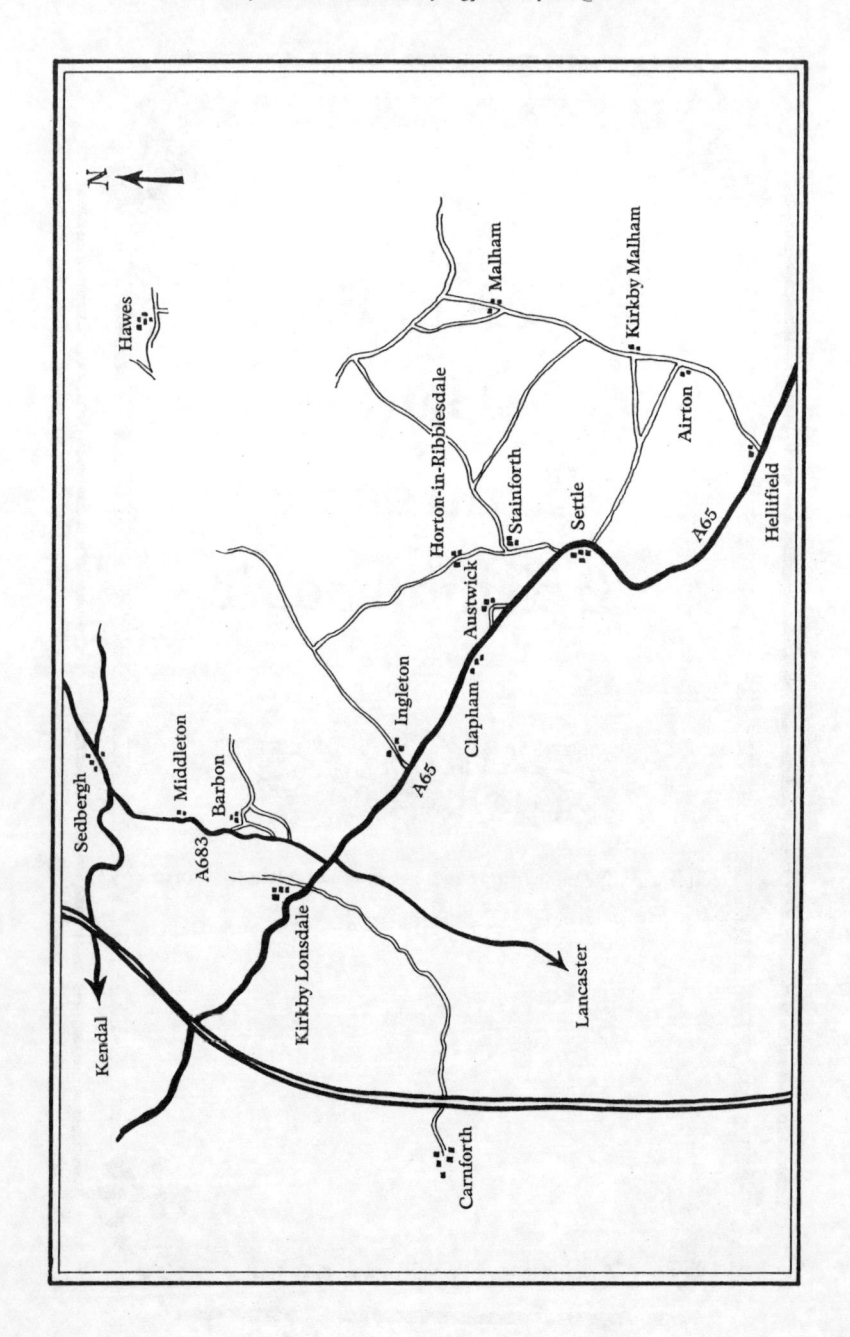

Ghost Trails of the Yorkshire Dales

Delightful Dent

Of all the valleys in the Yorkshire Dales, Dentdale is the one most likely to work its charm on the visitor. The valley is greener and more heavily wooded than any other. The highest point in the Yorkshire Dales - Whernside - dominates the head of the valley. Rise Hill, and Great Coum flank the small 'town', in which rows of ancient cottages seem to straddle the cobbled streets.

Barth Bridge, Dent

Dent is recorded as 'Denton' in Doomsday (1086). The ancient manor looked for its wealth to the 'good land' running alongside River Dee. Little has changed in the millennium. When the railway passed the valley at both ends, Dent was left almost untouched in the world that changed so rapidly elsewhere.

In summer Dent 'town' soaks up visitors like a sponge. But even the cavernous 'green' car park (provided by the National Park) can become log-jammed for special events such as the August Bank Holiday Monday Gala - a classic amongst traditional country fairs.

The 'town' has much to offer the visitor. Dent Stores is a lovely rural 'emporium', and the friendly staff at the Post Office may tempt you fill any spare space in the shopping basket. Artist John Cook's studio is well worth a visit, and Ben Lyon's 'outdoor' shop has much to offer the visitor who believes that legs are an asset in the countryside.

One of the loveliest walks in the Dales begins just above the 'town'. Or, as the legendary Wainwright put it : 'Aged and decrepit walkers whose powers are so reduced that they dare not contemplate the ascent of Great Coum, may at least enjoy its initial delights by a stroll up Flinter Gill and back again.'

Above Flinter Gill, Dent

Two excellent pubs provide inexpensive meals, as well the best locally brewed ales in the UK. Customers should be warned that the Ram's Bottom brew may seem innocuous, but has been known to lead to clumsy encounters with cobblestones.

Stone Close, a cafe which becomes a restaurant in the evening, offers the most imaginative menu for many a mile. It has rightly been dubbed 'the best little cafe in the Dales.'

There are two well-equipped campsites on the fringe of the 'town', and a wide variety of bed and breakfast style accommodation is scattered around the valley.

Father Of Geology

Dent's greatest son was the 19th. century 'father of geology' - Adam Sedgewick. Known locally as Adam o' the' Parsons (he was the son of the perpetual curate) his influence on the development of the science was considerable. He corresponded regularly with Queen Victoria and was favoured with a seat in her private box at the Coronation. His memorial is a fountain carved from a huge slab of Shap granite.

The Adam Sedgewick Memorial Fountain, Dent

The Dent Vampire

St. Andrew's Church is more than nine centuries old. The so-called vampire grave is at the entrance to the building. The stone slab records that George Hodgson died on June 4th. 1715 at the age of 91. Two thirds of the way up the slab is a circular dip in the stone. At the centre of the circle is the tip of a metal rod.

It is said that George rose from his grave and drank the blood of farm animals, and just possibly the odd tipple of warm human gore. Naturally enough, the good citizens of Dent were unhappy with this arrangement and made sure that George was firmly pinned in his coffin with a rod drilled through the stone slab above.

The story is improbable, but it raises a number of unanswered questions.

The parish record indicates that George Hodgson was merely 'a pauper of Dent's Town.' Why then should his body lie in the most favoured of positions before the church porch? Those who believe the vampire story make much of the fact that the grave was positioned where 'three paths meet.' They argue too that this was not the first burial place, but a site selected to help guarantee more permanent interment.

Little is known of George Hodgson the man. He married Elizabeth Greenbank in 1644, and a second wife, Barbary, outlived him by five years. His days can be reckoned alongside at least part of the reigns of six English monarchs, and the 11 years of the Commonwealth.

But longevity was not uncommon in the Hodgson family. A nephew, James lived to be 85. George's son, John, also achieved his ninth decade.

Those whose dismiss the vampire story, argue that a combination of senility, and pronounced canine teeth - a feature of later generations of Hodgsons - are frail foundations for a legend. It is also claimed that the metal rod in the tombstone is nothing more than the retaining pin for a (lost) inscription disc.

This all may be so, but it does not add up to a full explanation of the hysteria that followed his death. And then, there is still the question of the high profile pauper's grave...

There may be an answer.

Ten years earlier Richard Trotter of High Hall - Dent's premier citizen - had died.

In 1671, Richard and seven Dent yeomen had purchased the manor from the absentee landlord. In the years that followed Richard tried to buy up the rights and lands of the others. Despite heavy borrowing his intention was thwarted. This lead to a flurry of litigation and bad feeling. When Richard Trotter died in July 1705, his family claimed one final piece of real estate - the coveted burial plot at the church porch.

Another document reveals that in June 1685 Susanna Middleton, a child, was sent by her stepfather and tutor (Richard Bullman of Greyrigg) 'to table with John Hodgson of Dent Parish.' John was George Hodgson's son. A woman, called Jenet (Janet) Woodale accompanied the child.

We know that arrangements were made by one Will Atkinson of Dillicar to indemnity the Parish of Dent against the child's upkeep. In the same month Richard Trotter gave Atkinson a peppercorn tenancy.

Was Richard Trotter, or a member of his family, the natural father of Susanna Middleton? There are other connections which strengthen this possibility. Richard Bullman (the girl's stepfather) had formerly been tutor at High Hall, and John Hodgson was a retired stonemason who had worked on the Trotter estate. Both perhaps could be trusted to be discreet?

Had the Trotter name been protected by sending the dirty washing away from the valley? And did a new factor, such as the former tutor's infirmity, mean that fresh arrangements had be made?

Certainly the Hodgsons benefited from taking in the child. John was granted valuable rights of pasturage.

But by 1701 there had been a falling out. It began with a dispute about responsibility for maintaining a ford. Then there was a very public affray featuring Richard Trotter's son (also Richard) and Miles Hodgson - possibly John's nephew.

In the same year 16 year old Susanna Middleton left the Hodgson household to become a companion for Dorothy Trotter at High Hall.

When 16 years later the patriarch of the Hodgson family was laid to rest, we can be sure it was done in some style. And may there just have been a whiff if revenge in the air as the prosperous was swapped for the pauper? Could it just possible that the Hodgson family milked fear and superstition to make sure that the still despised Richard Trotter was evicted from his grave?

You will find little evidence of the once powerful Trotter name in the valley today. The Hodgsons however are still as much a part of Dent as the ancient cottages and cobblestones.

The Phantom Of Flood Lane

Flood Lane or 'Back Lane' is a loop of road that links the river bridges at each end of the 'town'.

The phantom is a 'white lady' apparition - mainly active around sunset on winter evenings. She appears when the lane is awash with flood water and vanishes almost as soon as she is seen.

It may be that this is the ghost of a former resident of Biggerside - a farmhouse that dates from the 17th. century. Tradition has it that the woman took food to her husband who was working close to the house, found him injured, and was swept away by the swollen river as she went for assistance.

The River Dee, at Dent

Literary Connections

Charles Kingsley, the author of The Water Babies (1863), a massively influential novel, made a research trip to Dent in 1858.

The book fostered the love of nature and drew attention to the worst excesses of child exploitation. Unhappily the sentimental, semi-parable style makes it almost unreadable today.

The Keswick poet, Robert Southey, referred to the 'Terrible Knitters of Dent.' There was nothing particularly frightening in the outward appearance of those involved in the cottage industry. 'Terrible' referred to their prodigious output.

By the time Southey made his observation the industry was already in decline : stockings were rapidly being replaced by long trousers.

There have also been claims made for a Bronte association with Dent. Two of the famous sisters (Charlotte and Emily) attended a school at Cowan Bridge near Kirkby Lonsdale. It is possible, perhaps even likely, that they were familiar with Dentdale. There is however no substantive proof of this.

A Phantom Punch-up

One of Dent's most remarkable characters was Elliner Brown - a famously strong man who was landlord of the (no longer existing) White Hart Inn.

This description of the man was written some years after his death in 1723.

'Elliner Brown believed that no conversation within the hostelry should exclude him. As he was a large man - of some twenty stones or more - there were few who sought to inhibit his entry into discourse. Although the strength in his arm was great, it was balanced by a weakness of intellect. Elliner provided the strongest ale in Dent and dispensed for profit that which he was unable to consume himself. He insulted his customers as purposefully as the blacksmith may fix iron shoes to his. Indeed, he was so known for it, and so vile in his manner, that many held him in special affection.'

Elliner Brown had a feud with rival landlord, George Guy, over the rights to a draw-well in the close by the George and Dragon. Whether or not this came to fisticuffs is not known, but the matter remained unresolved when Elliner died.

For more than a century there were those who claimed to witness a phantom punch-up between the two rivals. As George Guy did not expire for a further 25 years, it is perhaps assumed that Elliner waited patiently for the first round bell.

The Best Ale Under The Sun

The Sun Inn opened for business some time in 1758. The hostelry was built for John Brown on the site of a forge 'joined on the north side by another inn, and on the south by a brewhouse.'

John Brown, the first owner, was Elliner's son. This small hostelry has been consistently popular with both locals and visitors for two and a half centuries.

A Country Market

Market Fairs had traditionally been held fortnightly from mid-February until May.

A 19th. century account describes the scene around the square : ' The market at Dent's town had dwindled by 1830. Elderly people remember it being held 60 to 70 years earlier. Many carts converged on the town and farmer's wives laid butter on tables covered in white cloth in a barn near the George and Dragon. Promptly, at half-past-twelve the bellman cried 'draw up' 'draw up' around the town. It is remembered, in lieu of newspapers, the bellman standing on the mounting block of the George and Dragon, announcing the week's events as people came out of the church.'

Old And Infirm

A letter from a Victorian perpetual curate of Dent caused some head-scratching.

He complained to the bishop of being so old and infirm that he was unable to continue with his pastoral responsibilities. The bishop, probably noting the sturdy copper-plate writing, was at first unwilling to consider a resignation.

But the curate was however allowed to go, and was granted a pension by the 'statesmen' (or sidesmen) of Dent.

But another document perhaps hints at the truth. Some months before announcing his infirmity the married curate had received a substantial bequest from a local widow...

St Andrew's Church, Dent

Ghost Trails of the Yorkshire Dales

August Bank Holiday Gala, Dent

Dent Town

Leave Dent westwards and turn left at Gawthrop before taking the steep road upwards towards Kirkby Lonsdale.

Coining It In

The area around Middleton was once terrorised by the notorious Smorthwaite gang of Abbey Farm. Their crimes included robbery, clipping and coining, and sheep stealing. One of their most famous raids was on a local mint that had been established by Anthony Fawcett soon after the Restoration.

The gang managed to stay one step ahead of the law for many years. Finally the tide turned when a gang member, Edmund Bainbridge, turned king's evidence against Henry and William Smorthwaite.

The brothers must have known their days were numbered when the trial took place before the infamous Judge Jeffries. He handed down the predictable verdict. The brothers were hung at Lancaster on 8th. August 1684.

Late night interlopers around Barbon and Middleton have sometimes had an unpleasant surprise.

Faces At The Window

Occupants of cars parked at the roadside may not at first have been aware of a presence announced by grinding and rasping noises. Even the rhythmic rocking of the vehicle has sometimes been dismissed as eagerness within, rather than any external force. But hideous notes of laughter, and grotesque faces pushed up against the glass, are guaranteed to wreck even the most frenzied of passions.

Although the Smorthwaite name has been attached to this campaign of lust destruction, there is little evidence that this is the source of the phantom force. One oddity is that local lovers have either not been terror-targeted, or have been unwilling to discuss it. Victims are invariably warm weather wanderers from Kendal and Lancaster.

There is plenty of parking on both sides of Devil's Bridge at Kirkby Lonsdale. The town can be accessed by a footpath by the sports fields, or by following the riverside to the steep steps that rise to Ruskin's View

Lovely Lunesdale

The Lune Valley is different kind of England to the sheep country that makes up much of the Dales. Lush green fields and gentle undulations are the most common features of the landscape alongside the waters of Lune, Keer, Greta, and the Lupton Beck.

Kirkby Lonsdale is a lovely small market town. It is brimmed full of character and charm.

The Devil's Bargain

Devil's Bridge takes its name from a famous local legend. It is said that an old lady wanted to cross the river and found the ford too deep. The devil promised to build a bridge on the condition that he could claim the first creature that crossed as his own. As soon as the devil had completed his feat of engineering the old lady returned with a cake which she threw onto the bridge. A dog, sensing dinner no doubt, set off in pursuit...

The bridge is perhaps more likely to have been built by monks from Fountains Abbey to carry wool from their granges in the Lake District back to Yorkshire. There were grants of portage (tolls) in 1275 and 1365. Major repairs and improvements were carried out in the early 18th. century.

The Fairs

A Fair Charter was granted to Kirkby Lonsdale in 1227. The fair tradition is maintained by the lively Victorian Fair which is held each September. This is a splendid excuse for everyone to dress up.

There are still year-round markets, around the old market cross. The cross has been moved to what is still referred to as the horse market.

They Came To Kirkby

William Wordsworth recommended the view over the Lune to Turner who painted it. Ruskin later stood at the same place and called it 'one of the loveliest scenes in England'. The spot, which can be easily located behind the church, has therefore strangely acquired the title 'Ruskin's View', rather than perhaps 'Turner's Easel', or 'Wordsworth's Idea'?

Charlotte and Emily Bronte knew Kirkby Lonsdale well. They were sent to board at the nearby clergy school at Cowan Bridge. The austere building can be seen at the side of the A65.

Maria and Elizabeth Bronte, who also attended the school, died in 1824. Charlotte and Emily returned home to Howarth to be educated.

Kirkby Lonsdale later became the 'Lowton' of Charlotte's classic novel Jane Eyre. The early chapters provide a harrowing account of conditions at the school. Although this is a work of fiction there is no doubt that Charlotte believed that the rigorous regime, poor food and dreadful management, all contributed to the death of her sisters. Her own health, and that of sister Emily, were also affected.

In fairness it should be pointed out that Anne Bronte, the youngest of the literary sisters, who did not attend the school, died at age of 29. Emily, the genius who gave us 'Wuthering Heights' survived just 30 years. Charlotte wrote her four great novels during the last decade of her life. She died in childbirth less than a year after her marriage, and some months before her 40th. birthday.

A Capital Place

The 11th. century St. Mary's Church is well worth a visit. The building features fine stained glass and carved nave capitals.

St Mary's Church, Kirkby Lonsdale

The Seventh Queen

Molly Hall was a well-known local witch.

One evening, Tom Grinton the miller, and six of his friends were playing cards. In six successive hands Tom found that he held the Queen of Hearts. One of the other men was about to place a side bet that the same card would turn up in Tom's hand a seventh time, when Molly Hall put her head round the door.

First she instructed the man to put the coin pack in his pocket. Then she told Tom Grinton that he would indeed be dealt the card a seventh time.

The pack was shuffled and the cards were dealt, and sure enough the Queen of Hearts turned up in Tom's hand. This was a warning, said Molly, that he was about to suffer for cruelty to his lady friend.

Tom had two major interests - cards and chasing women. In both activities he had a track record of abject failure. But Tom was the persevering sort. There were two connected consequences : he was perpetually broke, and the one woman who was still prepared to forgive all transgressions was now well beyond the first flush of youth.

But the witch's warning pricked his conscience. He turned the hand over, made his apologies to the others, and prepared to leave. Molly told him this would make no difference - the cards were now stacked against him.

Molly Hall's reputation for witchery was well deserved. Her curses were considered to be even more vile than the recipe for her own authentic version of shepherd's pie.

Tom was so frightened that he fell on his knees and promised to marry the longsuffering Sarah Haygarth.

But again Molly told him that the seventh Queen of Hearts had sealed his fate and there was nothing she could do about it. But because of his penitence she would ask Lucifer to make his death less lingering and painful that it would otherwise have been.

Tom was now seriously upset. He ran as fast as he could to Sarah's cottage. He banged furiously on the door but there was no reply. He turned and ran towards their special meeting place - below the parapets of Devil's Bridge.

The rain was falling heavily now and the pale moonlight was masked by the clouds. He stumbled in the darkness as he approached the bridge, and called out Sarah's name. He thought perhaps he heard a reply and slid down the grassy bank to the water's edge. He called her name again. This time he was sure she was there - some way off in the rushing water.

He paddled out from the bank, slipped on a stone, and fell heavily into the torrent.

The next day, when the waters subsided, the two bodies were found in shallows at the island downstream. Sarah Haygarth had been dead for several hours longer than Tom Grinton. It was said that he had been playing cards when he heard of her suicide, and decided to share her fate in the deep peaty waters of the Lune.

From time to time when the rain sheets down on the water, dark figures have been seen battling against the force of the flow. But as the eye follows, these figures fade and dissolve in the fast flowing water.

Some call this a trick of the imagination. Others say it is a natural delusion created by the crests and crowns of the stream. But is it a coincidence that long ago in local parlance these crowns and crests were given rather different names?

They were called the King and Queen of Hearts.

Take the A65 towards Ingleton. Pass the Brontes School on the right at Cowan Bridge

Whooping It Up

Whoop Hall Inn, which dates from 1618, is linked with the ghost of a murdered coachman. From time to time shrieks and squeals have been heard in the vicinity.

Ghost Trails of the Yorkshire Dales

Lamentation

The lovely old Firthwhaite Park House can only be accessed from a private road.

A late 18th. century owner was noted as a man of exceptional cruelty. There were rumours that he was responsible for the disappearances of a number of children in the area, but nothing was proved.

But on cold winter nights it is claimed that the lamentation of young voices can be heard. In 1965 a whole troop of girl guides were reduced to hysteria by what was later described by their leader as 'the anguished cries of young voices.'

Firthwhaite Park House

Nine Falls

Ingleton is a noted centre for caves and waterfalls. The five mile circular walk (up the Doe and back down the Twiss) has been famous for two centuries. This is a 'granny walk' on well laid out paths, but it is not less impressive for that. The nine waterfalls, and Thornton Force in particular, are spectacular.

Thornton Force, Ingleton

The Sleeping Lion

Ingleton is dominated by the dozing-lion-shaped mass of Ingleborough. White Scar Caves, at the base of the hill, are popular with visitors.

The Terrible Tontine

The tontine was once popular in inheritance law. The principle of passing land or property to the last survivor - normally of brothers - was the legal enshrinement of the survival of the fittest. It also prevented the breaking up of a farm or estate, or the repeated ruination of death duties.

But the tontine is now outlawed. This is mainly because it was often a catalyst for murder.

Ghost Trails of the Yorkshire Dales

The Gatenby sisters of Ingleton are a case in point. Each was equally determined to win the prize after the death of their mother. Each planned to poison the other at the meal immediately after the funeral. Both were successful.

Unhappily this left a further legal wrangle, because the subsequent inheritance depended on proving which of the sisters had died first. The 'survivor' (albeit for just a few minutes) was technically the beneficiary of the tontine. The matter was further complicated because neither sister left a will. Ironically, as there were no close relatives they would (tontine apart) have stood to inherit from each other.

More than half of the value of the estate found its way into the hands of lawyers before a distant cousin was finally successful with her claim.

Perhaps this begins to explain Ingleton's once famous spectral attraction.

The two ghostly sisters were regularly seen chasing each other around the village in a macabre game of hide and seek.

The game, in the best traditions of haunting, was said to begin as the church clock struck midnight. It ended when each sister in turn had successfully located the other's hiding place. Then both would decorously adjust their winding sheets and return quietly to the churchyard.

Tradition has it that the ghostly game was played twice weekly (Wednesdays and Saturdays) for seven years and seven months. By sheer coincidence, it seems, this was exactly the time it took for the inheritance to be settled.

It is possibly less of a coincidence that the story almost certainly originates from Dales diarist, the Reverend William Pierce. His is probably the first (1674), and possibly the only near-contemporary account of the grisly Gatenby sisters.

It may be seen by sceptics as no coincidence at all that the Reverend Pierce had a pathological hatred of lawyers.

Take the A65 and turn off for Clapham

Growing In Popularity

The growing popularity of Clapham as a centre means it has changed almost beyond recognition in recent years.

The National Park Information Centre is blessed with exceptionally friendly and knowledgeable staff. The parking area is more than adequate parking even in the busier months.

Clapham now has five tea rooms, a fair range of bed and breakfast accommodation, and an imaginatively stocked gift shop

High Spirits

High Clapdale Farm is said to feature a White Lady apparition. For many years the property was leased by the University of Lancaster and the ghost is claimed to have made regular appearances.

Many of these materialisations seem to have coincided with students returning late in the evening, by all accounts in suitably high spirits themselves.

Turned On

Clapham was one of the first villages in the UK to have electric street lighting.

Farrer's Cave And Trail

The botanist, Reginald Farrer of Ingleborough Hall, created the Himalayan landscape that leads to the cave. The gentle ascent of a little more than a mile which features exotic plants from the

Alps, Japan, and Tibet. It is best seen at rhododendron time in late May and June.

Clapham has probably the best show cave in the Dales. It's relatively out-of-the-way position means it is also the least frequently visited. It was discovered by Farrer in 1837, and the first section was laid out to make it 'most accessible for the visitor.'

A legendary local figure will forever be associated with the cave. This is Peter Shaw - known to all as 'Chester'. He did not allow the loss of a leg to end his caving career, and for many years he shared the spotlight with his constant canine companion, Domino.

Until the late 1980's, when he called it a day, there were always two types of visit to the Clapham cave. An ordinary guided visit was excellent : a Chester tour was unforgettable.

Gaping Ghyll

Gaping Ghyll is on the Ingleborough ascent above the cave.

The first descent into the chasm was made by the Frenchman, Martell, in 1885. Martell is best remembered for discovering Padirac - near Rocamador - which for more than a century has been Europe's premier show cave.

For Gaping Ghyll he used the same basic equipment - a rope ladder and a lantern fixed to his arm.

Unlike Padirac, Gaping Ghyll is not normally accessible to the public. At summer bank holiday however, a stream is diverted and a chair-winch makes the descent possible.

The 360 foot drop makes the waterfall the UK's highest unbroken drop. The chasm below is of Cathedral proportions. It is a magnificent starting point for those intrepid enough to explore many miles of underground passages.

Gaping Ghyll, August Bank Holiday

Bones Of Contention

In 1947 a skeleton was found on a ledge in the Great Chamber. There was no evidence of a skull, but the legs had been clearly forced up into the body which suggested a heavy fall.

As a large speleological team had conducted a major exploration of the cave the previous year, it is not likely that the skeleton had been there at that time. The remains were never identified.

A second skeleton was found at Trow Ghyll in the same year. In this case the skull was intact, but much of the rest of the skeleton was missing. Coins found nearby were dated no older than 1944. Again the remains were not identified.

Some fairly fanciful theories forge links between the two suspicious deaths. None of them are entirely satisfactory. It is perhaps more probable that these were two entirely independent accidents or incidents, connected only by the odd coincidence of time.

A Special Intuition

One of the greatest dangers of potholing is heavy rain swelling water levels in the cave systems. Those who are underground for a long time are particularly likely to lose track of weather conditions outside. Certain caverns are notorious for flooding quickly and fatalities in the sport are all too frequent.

In late August 1946, brothers David and Denis Hutton were members of a team of seven exploring one of the remoter corridors of the Gaping Ghyll system. The forecast had been close to ideal. No rain was anticipated for at least 72 hours.

As often happens in the Dales, the forecast can be wrong. On this occasion the rain started intermittently, then turned to torrents.

The party became trapped in a narrow gallery, perched above the water level, but unable to move. When the seven failed to surface the alarm was raised, but the rescue party were forced to wait until the waters subsided. As the hours ticked away, there were dark thoughts of disaster.

But all was well. The seven were brought out exhausted, but unharmed. Much of this was said to be down to the 'intuition' of one of the rescuers who seemed to know exactly where to locate the stranded seven.

He was Jeb Thomas. Jeb was well-known to all the rescuers as a hugely competent caver.

But as soon as the rescue was completed, Jeb disappeared. Denis Hutton takes up the story

" Cave rescue was less systematic in those days. Half a dozen frantic phone-calls started it. The 'bush telegraph' did the rest. You never knew quite who was going to turn up.

" Jeb was a well-liked character. He'd been caving since before the war. Not one of the great pioneers perhaps, but he was well respected by the caving fraternity. Even when he came home on leave he could hardly wait to go caving or climbing.

" Jeb had a thin wiry frame, but I reckon he could more than punch his weight. But his eyes weren't good. That's why he 'sailed a desk' during the war. He'd never admit to the problem, but you'd often see him squinting.

" But he had this kind of seventh sense. He seemed to know the geography of a system instinctively. I've even known him anticipate a rock fall. He was the one who found us. I'm told he came more or less straight to us, which is amazing. We'd left a 'plan of campaign' at the hotel, but we hadn't stuck to it. Part of the reason was the panic that set in when the flooding began. We'd started back, changed our minds, then taken refuge in a side gallery.

" The fact that they reached us so swiftly made a big difference. There was only one minor injury, but we'd lost some equipment and had been more than 12 hours without food. We'd seen the water level falling, and had just made up are minds to try to battle our way our way out. Then Jeb arrived with reinforcements.

" I wrote to him afterwards. I said I owed him a beer or two. But there was no reply.

" About twelve months later I was down in Derbyshire. That was Jeb's neck of the woods. I was chatting to some fellow cavers one night when the subject of the rescue came up. That took the conversation to Jeb.

" It went quiet. Then somebody told me Jeb had died. He'd been killed on a climbing jaunt in the Ardeche the previous year. He'd just fallen from the face. Nobody seemed to know why.

" I remember muttering something about it being late in the season.

" One of them, a giant of a man called Moss Tully, shrugged his shoulders. Moss didn't know the exact date of the accident, but Jeb's body had been brought back home for burial. That had taken some time. Lots of red tape apparently.

" Moss had been to the funeral, then he adjourned for a pint or two with the local caving crew.

" And there was something odd about the wake. Daft really, but Moss remembered there'd been no sandwiches. Crazy isn't it? But he was sure it had something to do with rationing. But hadn't bread rationing been introduced several weeks before the cave rescue?

" Wires were crossed somewhere. I had to find out, and I did.

" Moss Tully had been right. In fact Jeb's funeral had taken place on the very day bread rationing was introduced - July 22nd. 1946. That was four and a half weeks before the rescue at Gaping Ghyll."

The Austwick Cuckoos

Close to Clapham is Austwick. The village features a fine Elizabethan fortified manor house, and 17th. century cottages around the small green.

For many years the good people of Austwick have suffered the regional equivalent of the Irish joke. The village is sometimes called Cuckoo Town. The story is that the villagers captured and caged a cuckoo one autumn. The theory was that the bird was associated with the coming of better weather. If he could not escape then wouldn't they enjoy a mild winter?

It is said that they build a special fence to keep the fog at bay. Records sadly do not indicate whether or not this was successful...

The logic of Austwick men - known as Carles - was equally demonstrated by the carrying of a whittle - a kind of knife used by the shepherding community to cut meat. It is said that one of the Austwick 'Carles' was high on the hills and determined to leave the whittle in a place where it could be easily retrieved. There were no trees or distinctive rocks in the area, so he hid the knife in the shadow created by a cloud.

It is said that another of the 'Carles' decided to take a wheelbarrow to Clapham by the shortest route. This meant lifting the barrow and contents over two dozen stiles.

Yet another 'Carle' found a piece of cheese in a pool and valiantly attempted to lift it out of the water. Despite his best efforts he was defeated. But worse was to follow. The cheese vanished altogether when a cloud passed in front of the moon.

Perhaps the most famous story of all concerns the 'Carle' who had his corn ravaged by woodpigeons. He organised a shooting party, only to find that the birds flew away. Not to be defeated the man came up with a superior sort of plan. He bent the barrel of a gun in such a way that he could hide behind a tree and still reduce the woodpigeon population. Unhappily the bend in the barrel was too great and the unfortunate man returned to the village with buttocks weighed down with lead shot.

The stories are of course apocryphal. But it is said that some of the sweetest deals in the Dales have been down to the 'Carles' of Austwick. Creating the impression of stupidity can sometimes be an asset in business. There is little doubt that successive generations of 'Carles' have been happy to sustain the myth.

Take the A65 towards Settle, turning off the major road at Giggleswick

Mist And Myth

The village of Giggleswick is noted for the lovely church dedicated to St. Alkelda. The present building dates mainly from the 15th. century but there is some evidence of Saxon origins.

The church is perpendicular with a fine carved pulpit (1680) and an ancient reading desk. An 'invasion beam' is tucked into the thickness of the wall. The idea was to pull it across the door and fix it into a socket on the opposite wall.

When the village was threatened many of the local population would have taken refuge in the building.

Alkelda was very likely a woman of noble Saxon birth. It is said that she suffered martyrdom by strangulation. One tradition has it that she was strangled with a scarf, another with her own long hair. In both versions the villains were Norse women.

The saint is, to say the least, a misty historical figure. She is not mentioned in the Finchdale or Anglo-Saxon Chronicles. Indeed the first written reference occurs as late as the 13th. century, though martyrdom can hardly have taken place any later than the 10th. The earliest Giggleswick record of her name appears in a will of 1528.

There are even scholarly arguments about the name. Perhaps the most likely possibility is that Alkelda is a corruption of the Old English word ' haelingkeld', which means holy well. There are holy wells next to both churches dedicated to the saint. The other is at Middleham where it is said the saint is buried.

The tradition that Alkelda performed baptisms at Giggleswick's Ebbing and Flowing Well confuses matters further. The well is primarily associated with pre-Christian belief.

As there is no solid historical foundation for the existence of the saint, the temptation is to bracket her along with Saint George as an inspiring element of folklore. It both cases there is an inheritance of veneration almost certainly taken from pagan tradition. More specifically, for both these shadowy saints there is a clear attachment to the common Aryan myth of the sun-god as the conqueror of powers of darkness.

Ebb And Flow

The Ebbing and Flowing Well can be located above the village on Giggleswick Scar. The water literally ebbs and flows several times a day without any wholly satisfactory explanation.

It is said that a nymph being pursued by an over-amorous satyr prayed to the gods for help. They turned her into the spring which ebbs and flows with her breathing.

The story was almost certainly Christianised into the Alkelda baptisms. The links include the obsession with purity (symbolised by the water and nymph) and the shadowy virgin saint.

Michael Drayton, an early 17th. century poet whose work rivals that of William McGonagall for awfulness, penned verses on the subject which begin :

In all my spacious tract, let them so wise survey
My Ribble's rising banks, their worst, and let them say,
At Giggleswick, where I a fountain can you show
That eight times a day is said to ebb and flow.
There sometimes was a nymph, and in the mountains high
Of Craven, whose blue heads for caps put on the sky...

Nevinson's Leap

It is said that the 17th. century highwayman, John Nevinson, evaded capture in these parts after letting his horse drink at the well.

The water rekindled the animals strength and Nevinson was able to conjure a mighty leap from the top of the cliff. His pursuers were less than keen to similarly risk their necks so the highwayman escaped.

The place where this occurred is still called Nevinson's Leap. A ghostly version of the event is said to occur each anniversary. Unhappily, 'witnesses' cannot agree on the date.

Tucked Up In Bed

The famous public school was founded in 1507. In more recent years that most amiable of TV personalities, Russell Harty, taught at the school before beginning his successful media career. Russell Harty became one of the first well-known victims of AIDS.

Giggleswick School

The school is noted for more than the quality of education it provides.

The challenging voice of a former housemaster is said to be heard around the corridors at night. The diligent intent of this scholarly shade is to ensure that the school's boarders are all snugly snoring in their dormitories.

Malicious gossip has it that the story is no more than a propaganda exercise on behalf of the school's authorities. After all, fear has long been a potent tool of discipline.

Follow the old A65 road into Settle

Settle Sights

Settle has had a market since 1249. Each Tuesday this small market town comes alive as it becomes the focus of the wider community. The shambles buildings help to create much of the mood of the past. The ground floor areas were formerly slaughter houses.

A French style town hall (1832) is sited near the old tollbooth. The building features a watchman's room and an old-fashioned lock-up. The so-called 'Pig Jury' used to meet here to regulate trading at fairs and markets.

Preston's Folly dates from 1679. A project that began on a grand scale with mock-tudor masonry and mullioned windows came to a premature end when Thomas Preston ran out of cash.

The Museum of North Craven life is of particular interest to those with a special interest in geology and early settlements. The museum also admirably sketches the development of farming, trades, and communications.

The Coronation Hoard

On the day of Queen Victoria's coronation (May 1838), Micheal Horner was walking a friend's dog through the hillside scree in Langcliffe Scar when he discovered a cave entrance. The 'Victoria Cave' has since yielded very important insights into the remoter past of Upper Ribblesdale. Finds trace back in time from Roman brooches to the bones of arctic fox, bear, elephant, hippopotamus, hyena, mammoth and reindeer. There are also ornaments, utensils and weapons associated with Mesolithic hunters and the Iron Age. Many of these discoveries are now in the British Museum.

Great Expectations

The town is associated with a spectral coach and four. This is driven by a son of the 4th. Earl of Northumberland, confusingly called 'Sir Percy' because of the family name.

The 4th. Earl - Henry - had turned Yorkist during the Wars of the Roses. Nevertheless he refused to fight for Richard III at Bosworth (August 22nd. 1485) and later managed to find favour with Henry VII.

There has been no reported sighting of the spectral coach since September 3rd. 1885. At that time it was still said to contain members of the Earl's family escaping the wrath of the Yorkist rebels. There were great expectations in September 1985 - the 500th. anniversary of the event. But despite the prepared welcome of Lancaster University's 'Ghostwatch Team' - no coach, horses, or Percys put in an appearance.

Forging A Connection

Another supernatural event with equestrian connections dates back a mere three and a half centuries.

Tom Cononley was a blacksmith who was stabbed in a brawl at a stable in Long Preston in 1652. He died at home in Settle 11 days later. The crash of hammer on anvil has been heard outside the old smithy - now a market place cafe - on many occasions.

You Can't Take It With You

Old Naked Man Cafe, Settle

Ye Old Naked Man Cafe was once a (17th. century) coaching inn. The odd motif - a naked man in his coffin - is said to be a former landlord's protest against the preoccupation with fashion at the time. It is just possible though that this was a subtle form of advertising. A similar encoded message (at York) was translated as : 'You come into the world naked and leave it naked. So, as you can't take it with you, why not spend some of it here?'

There was once a Naked Lady at nearby Langcliffe - a once infamous hostelry. The influential Dawson family forced the closure of the establishment after the murder of the last licensee in the 19th. century.

Turn right approximately 100 metres south of the town centre. Pass the railway station on the left and follow the road through the industrial estate. Turn left towards Rathmell. A swift left right manoeuvre is required to cross the A65. Follow the minor roads to Rathmell, Long Gill and Tosside

Coming To Grief

From time to time the vision of a young woman has been picked out in car headlights near the packhorse bridge.

As the woman is standing in the middle of the road, facing the oncoming traffic, evasive action has to be taken. It is hardly surprising that a number of motorists have come to grief here.

This low-lying area of Upper Ribblesdale is particularly prone to stream mist - a possible explanation for the apparition.

Victims Of War

But if this is indeed a haunting, there is a story to fit the bill.

In the days that followed the First World War Armistice, a young Tosside woman waited anxiously for news of her husband. It has been said that the farming community suffered less heavily than most in a war which killed the most uniformed men in history. But she had already known the grief of losing three brothers and an uncle. Perhaps her fears as she waited were tinged with excitement, as she was now certain that an addition to the family was on the way.

Then the blow came in the shape of the familiar black-bordered envelope. Her husband was reported as missing in action just two days before hostilities ended.

Overcome with grief, she set off to break the news to her mother. Perhaps tears clouded her vision, for as she walked along the open road she did not see the straw-laden wagon bearing down on her.

She survived the accident but lost the baby. A few months later when a winter's chill turned to pneumonia she was all too willing to give up the fight.

There was a first sighting of the ghostly figure near the packhorse bridge a few weeks later. And on several of the occasions that the phenomenon has been reported since, a long grey coat has been mentioned.

On that cold November night in 1918 the distressed young woman had left home wearing a grey coat.

Join the B6478 for Wigglesworth and Long Preston. Turn briefly northwards for the village centre

The Ghost Deterrent

The Boar's Head is at the side of the busy A65 in Long Preston. It was in this building, formerly a stable, that Tom Cononley was stabbed in a brawl in 1652. A century later the first licensee of the Boar's Head opened the doors of this fine hostelry to the public. Indeed, the names of every landlord are recorded on a plaque nearby.

One former licensee hung himself in the cellar. A photograph, said to be of the man's mother, hangs in the bar. There were reports of a haunting at once time, but it is said that as long as the picture remains the ghost will not return.

Locals have been known to suggest that the picture has been misidentified. The reason the ghost has gone to ground, the say, is because the austere looking lady in the picture is the landlord's mother-in-law.

Turn south along the A65 for Hellifield

Hellifield would be a hot favourite in an Ugliest Village in the Dales competition.

The signposted road to Airton and Malham is at the south end of the village

The Devil And The Plump Incumbent

An odd 'incident' at Kirkby Malham is said to have occurred around the time of the accession of Queen Victoria.

The story is that the vicar and a young boy received an invitation to a banquet to hosted by Lucifer. The feast was neatly laid out on a family tombstone in the churchyard.

The Devil chose 'De Profundis' for the grace, and asked the vicar if this was appropriate for a banquet for the dead. The corpulent clergyman, whose attention was entirely on the spread, nodded approval and asked for the salt.

Both Devil and feast disappeared.

'De Profundis' is the Latin title of the 130th. psalm. This begins:

'Out of the deep I have called to thee O Lord. Hear my voice. O let thine ears consider well the voice of my complaint...'

The 'incident' appears to be a kind of ecclesiastical joke. Why this should be particularly linked to Kirkby Malham is uncertain. One theory is that a meaning can be found in the schism that surrounded Edward Harcourt, the Archbishop of York.

Harcourt was enthroned in 1807. But In 1831, this cousin of the last Lord Harcourt became the unlikely inheritor of Oxfordshire estates worthy of their Plantagenet pedigree. He also clearly prepared to limit his odds of entering the Pearly Gates to passing through the proverbial eye of the needle.

The lifestyle of the UK's wealthiest clergyman came under close scrutiny. Those who toadied to him were regarded with particular disdain in this 'fundamentalist' corner of Yorkshire. Many stories of feast and flatulence were circulated, and corruption was often seen as the bedfellow of every broad-beamed clergyman.

It is not unlikely that the plump incumbent of Kirkby Malham was regarded with suspicion, and that the story was invention to discredit him.

A Watery Grave

The churchyard also features the grave of a sea captain and his wife. It is said that she hated his long absences at sea, but agreed that they should also be separated in death by water.

The intention was to have her resting place on one side of a stream and his on the other. However, when the time came to dig her grave the rock proved to be a serious problem. Finally it was decided to place her coffin on his. But the already prepared (now faded) inscription reads : 'As the water parted us in life, so shall it in death.'

Continue on the minor road to Malham

Magnificent Malham

Craven country has captured hearts and minds for centuries. Charles Kingsley was a guest of Walter Morrison at Malham Tarn House (now a field study centre) in 1858. Malham Cove became the home of 'The Water Babies.'

The National Park Information Centre is at the south end of the village. Although car parking provision is generous there can occasionally be a problem at peak weekends. Malham receives more than half a million visitors a year.

Malham Cove is a 300 foot high natural amphitheatre out of which the River Aire flows. This follows the line of the Mid-Craven fault. Two and a half centuries ago the waterfall was higher than Niagara. The cove is topped by a splendid limestone pavement.

Malham Cove, detail

Erosion, in and around the cove, has been controlled largely through the efforts of the National Park itself and a small army of volunteer conservationists.

Hare Today...

It is said that a group of huntsmen once spotted a large hare in a field close to the cove. The horses and dogs gave chase, and the jaws of the lead dog snapped at the hare as it leapt a wall. The hare escaped but the dog's teeth had pulled out a small section of fur.

One of the huntsmen dismounted, climbed the wall, and looked over. There was no hare ; just an old woman rubbing her head which had a circle of hair missing.

The limestone pavement, Malham Cove

From Malham take the minor road to join the B6479 before Helwith Bridge. Pass through Selside, then on to Ribblehead

A Wonder Of Engineering

Ribblehead Viaduct is rated as one of the Seven Wonders of the Railway World. 7000 men worked on the 3 million Settle-Carlisle Railway. There are 21 viaducts and 14 tunnels. The tunnels were dug by candle-light. The deepest are more than 500 feet below ground.

The battle for the survival of the line began in earnest in 1983. It was won as much through holes in closure documentation as the enthusiasm of the thousands who supported the survival of this classic line.

The soggy foundations of the Ribble Head Viaduct, and the massive expense of making it safe, was a particular problem for the railway's supporters. But for those privileged to ride the rail below the mighty slopes of Whernside will tell you it was money well spent.

A brief diversion westwards along the B6255 brings you to Chapel-le-Dale

The Cost Of Rail Transport

The churchyard of St. Leonards at Chapel-le-Dale contains the graves of more than 100 workers who were victims of the perilous engineering project. This is the tip of the iceberg. It is estimated that thousands were killed, or seriously injured, in creating the 72 miles of the Settle-Carlisle railway.

This part of the Dales can seem harsh and even frightening. Daniel Defoe, who visited the area in 1720, wrote : ... 'Nor were the hills high and formidable only, but that had an inhospitable terror in them, all barren and wild...'

There is no need to talk of ghosts here.

Retrace your route eastwards along the B6255. Turn off for Dent near the summit of Gayle Moor.

A Delightful Descent

The descent into Dentdale is one of the greatest driving delights of the Dales. The bleakness of the high moor slowly gives way to the greenness of the valley below. You cross and re-cross the River Dee on the way to Dent's 'town'.

Dentdale View towards the Howgills

Dubbed By The Past

The Sportsman's Inn above Cowgill is well worth a visit. Although the old building was substantially modernised in the 1980's, the essential character has been retained. The original Sportman's Inn was the parlour of a neighbouring farm - Cow Dub. Though still known locally as 'The Dub', the present building has been in use since the end of the 18th. century.

The Wailing

At one time there was a fair amount of business conducted by a few local families in the slave markets of Liverpool. It is said that a former owner of 'The Dub' purchased an attractive female negro whose duties extended beyond domestic chores.

Inevitably she became pregnant. The owner locked her away in the cellar, and turned to the bottle for consolation. This lead to the poor woman's neglect and eventual death.

Although no haunting has been reported in recent years, it is said that the sound of wailing could be heard in various parts of the building until an exorcism was conducted in 1909.

Follow the road to Dent through the hamlets of Lea Yeat and Cowgill

Ghost Trails of the Yorkshire Dales

Historical Notes/glossary

A number of important sites and personages are referred to only in passing in the main body of the text. These notes are intended to remedy that omission for those seeking greater clarification of historical contexts.

The information is arranged alphabetically.

ARTHUR, KING OF THE BRITONS (?460 - ?515) Legendary Romano-British leader associated with a series of battles to repel the Anglo-Saxon invaders. Little is truly known of him, though his existence is now generally accepted. The medieval legends that persist are almost certainly just that.

BANNOCKBURN, BATTLE OF In June 1314 Edward II (qv) led an army of 20,000 men to relieve Stirling Castle. Robert the Bruce intercepted them with a much smaller force and the English came second.

BEDE, THE VENERABLE (673 - 735) A monk of Jarrow, Northumbria, he became famous during his lifetime for his writings on science and scripture. His single most famous work, however, is probably his Ecclesiastical History of the English People.

BENEDICTINES Name given to monks and nuns from the Roman Catholic Order of St. Benedict. Also known as the Black Monks. Equally famous for their learning and the liqueur named after them and still produced at a monastery near Fecamp in France.

BLACK DEATH (1348 - 1351) A name coined in Victorian England for an outbreak of bubonic plague which decimated the population of Britain. Its long term effect was to aid the breakdown the feudal system, by increasing the wages and hence the power, of the labouring classes.

BOWDLER, THOMAS (1754 -1825) A doctor who wielded his scalpel to Shakespeare(qv) taking out all those words which he considered improper. He tried the same operation on Gibbon's Decline & Fall of the Roman Empire, reducing that great tome to the size of a penny dreadful.

BOSWORTH FIELD, BATTLE OF (1485) Final battle of the Wars of the Roses (qv) which lead to the death of Richard III (qv) and the beginning of the Tudor Dynasty. The battle turned on the refusal of one of Richard's divisions - under the Percys of Northumberland - to fight.

BRONTES, CHARLOTTE, EMILY & ANNE Three Yorkshire novelist sisters who lived during the first half of the 19th century.

BURKE & HARE (Dates uncertain) Infamous grave robbers and murderers who operated in Edinburgh from 1827, selling corpses to medical schools. Hare turned King's Evidence and helped Burke to the scaffold.

CHARLES I, KING OF GREAT BRITAIN (1625 - 1649 B. 1600) Lack of honesty, political foresight, military and administrative competence and marriage to a Catholic princess, Henrietta Maria (qv) led to civil war (qv), in which he came second, and a date with an axeman in Whitehall. Unfortunate as it might have been for him, his death was the ultimate saviour of the Monarchy in Britain as it divided the Parliamentarians.

CISTERCIANS Name given to stricter offshoot of the Benedictines (qv). Also known as the White Monks. Best known as sheep farmers.

CIVIL WAR, THE ENGLISH (1642 - 1651) More properly called the Civil Wars. The culmination of the deterioration in the relationship between the crown and the parliament through the reigns of James I and Charles I (qv) and the financial and religious policies of Charles in particular, triggered rebellion in Scotland and Ireland.

The Short and Long Parliaments of 1640 demanded reform which included parliamentary control over the king's choice of advisors. In January 1642 Charles failed to secure the arrest of five members of Parliament and quit the capital. He set up his standard at Nottingham in August of the same year. The royalists enjoyed early success in battles at Edgehill, Newcastle and Hopton, but failed to consolidate these victories. Scottish troops under Argyll entered England and contributed to the first parliamentary success at Marston Moor. Argyll's troops were withdrawn to deal with a royalist uprising in Scotland and an indecisive battle was fought at Newbury.

In 1645 Fairfax's New Model Army inflicted a major defeat on the royalists at Naseby. In 1648 revolts in the south anticipated further intervention by the Scots on the king's behalf. Fairfax crushed the rebellion in the south and Cromwell defeated the invading Scots at Preston. Charles was tried by a court set up by the Rump Parliament and executed on 30th. January 1649.

In 1650 Cromwell (qv) inflicted a final defeat on the Scots at Dunbar, and in the following year Charles II's invading army was crushed at Worcester. The Commonwealth formed to govern the country at the end of the war lasted until Booth's Rising and the Restoration of 1660.

COMMONWEALTH (1649 - 1660) Title given to the period of English history when its ruler(s) were not royal. See Civil War.

CRECY, BATTLE OF (1346) English archers under Edward III against French cavalry under Philip VI. The French came a very poor second.

CROMWELL, THOMAS, EARL OF ESSEX. (1485 - 1540)
A clever schemer, he continued to find favour with Henry VIII (qv) after the downfall of his master, Cardinal Wolsey. He drafted the legislation that seceded the Church of England from Rome, thereby gaining Henry a divorce from Katherine of Aragon. Later he masterminded the dissolution of the monasteries which led to the Pilgrimage of Grace (qv). His downfall came because he was the chief negotiator who secured Anne of Cleves as a wife for Henry. Another Tudor victim of trumped up charges, he was executed for treason.

CROMWELL, OLIVER (1599 - 1658) Represented Huntingdon in the parliament of 1628 and Cambridge in the Short and Long Parliaments. He was 43 at the outbreak of the Civil War and in three years rose from the rank of captain to lieutenant-general. He created and moulded a superb cavalry force and replaced Fairfax as lord-general in 1650. He defended the Commonwealth at Dunbar and Worcester and became Lord Protector and Head of State in 1653. Despite his reforming zeal and expert military leadership, Oliver Cromwell is best remembered for the warts on his face and as the prime mover in the trial and execution of King Charles I.

DEFOE, DANIEL (1660 - 1731) Began his working life as a banker, switched to journalism, ended up a novelist and managed to be imprisoned for writing sedition in between. Led a busy life.

DEVONSHIRE, DUKES OF. Charles II was pleased to promote William Cavendish to a dukedom. However, upon hearing where the bulk of Cavendish lands were, he refused to dub William Duke of Derbyshire saying that he knew of no such place, and named the dukedom after somewhere he had heard of.

EDWARD II (1307 - 1327. Born 1284) Edward's reign was punctuated by famine, failures in war and baronial opposition. His extravagance and homosexuality made him unpopular, but the murder of a favourite (Gaveston) in 1312 destroyed the united face of the opposition. He suffered humiliating defeats at Bannockburn (qv) and in France and new opposition grew around Roger and Isabella Mortimer. Edward was deposed and brutally murdered in September 1327.

EDWARD IV (1461 - 1470, 1471 - 83. Born 1442.) A brave and popular soldier during the Wars of the Roses (qv). He won a significant victory at Towton (qv), but his marriage to Elizabeth Woodville alienated his mentor, Warwick the Kingmaker. He was driven into exile but returned to lead a successful campaign in March 1471. He gave England domestic peace but failed to reconcile disputes at court. The most important of these, between the Woodvilles and the Duke of Gloucester (the future Richard III) caused further strife after his death.

EDWARD VI, KING OF ENGLAND (1547 - 1553 b. 1537). Son of Henry VIII and Jane Seymour, Edward was an ardent Protestant and was much influenced by the Dukes of Somerset and Northumberland. It is possible that he initiated the plot to proclaim Lady Jane Grey Queen in place of his half-sister Mary, who was a Catholic. His other half sister, Elizabeth, (qv) was a Protestant, too.

ELIOT, GEORGE (1819 - 1890) Born Mary Evans but was forced to adopt male pseudonym in order to get published. During her lifetime she was possibly better known for her adulterous liaison with a married man.

ELIZABETH I (Queen of England 1558 - 1603. Born 1533) In 1536 her mother, Anne Boleyn, was executed in the Tower on the order of her father, Henry VIII. Elizabeth herself was imprisoned in the Tower during the reign of her half-sister, Mary.

Her political astuteness helped her not only to survive, but to become one of England's most celebrated monarchs. Her reign brought peace, and a measure of religious settlement until the War with Spain in 1585. The scuttling of the Armada settled that conflict, but revolts in Ireland and the Earl of Essex's rebellion were symptoms of unresolved difficulties. These seeds of discontent culminated in Civil War of 1642 and the end of absolute monarchy in Britain.

ERIC BLOODAXE, KING OF NORTHUMBRIA (Died 954) A son of Harald Finehair, King of Norway, Eric was born, and possibly died, a pagan. Yet one cleric, Archbishop Wulfstan, had joined with other notables of the day to make him king and another wrote sympathetically of his death at Stainmore, following treachery. It is certain, too, that sometime between 952 and his death he visited Cuthbert's shrine.

He was king twice. Once, for possibly only a few months around 947 and then again from 951 to 954. A strong ruler and warrior, he also appears to have been well liked and would undoubtedly be at the head of any 'Home Rule for Northumbria' movement, were he alive today.

FAWKES, GUY (1570 - 1606) Mercenary and fall guy for those wishing to rid the country of James I and re-introduce a Catholic monarchy.

FLODDEN, BATTLE OF (1513) Scottish invaders came second to English defenders in mass slaughter.

GREAT FIRE OF LONDON (1666) Began in Pudding Lane and destroyed 80% of London. Least known for stopping the plague outbreak that had struck the previous year.

HENRIETTA MARIA (1609 - 69) Queen consort of Charles I. Her influence over Charles - and her Catholicism - added to Charles' troubles to the point where he lost his head.

HENRY V (King of England 1413 - 1422. Born 1387) The first king to be fully literate in English. He claimed the French throne and embarked with an expeditionary force across the channel. He marched on Calais and won a famous victory at Agincourt in 1415. After diplomatic manoeuvring, he advanced through Normandy capturing Caen, Falaise and Rouen. After forming an important political alliance with Armagnac he carried on his triumph at Troyes (1420). He contracted dysentery during the siege at Meaux and died on 31st. August 1422 at the age of 35.

HENRY VII (1485 - 1507. Born 1457) First monarch of the Tudor Dynasty, Henry had a very dodgy claim to the throne of England through his mother Margaret Beaufort. The Beauforts were descended from Edward III through his son John of Gaunt, who luckily married his mistress and legitimised their children. A series of unfortunate deaths during the Wars of the Roses (qv) left him as the main champion of the Lancastrian side. He won.

HENRY VIII (1509 - 47. Born 1491) Henry came to the throne with little political or governmental experience. He learned these skills quickly and presided over one of the most lavish and cultured courts in Europe. His decision to divorce Katherine of Aragon created a division with Rome and the establishment of the Church of England. He was always the final power in government but had little taste for administration. This was left to famous servants, notably the three Thomas' - More, Cromwell (qv) , and Wolsey - all of whom suffered considerably after falling from the king's favour. Henry is now best remembered for his six wives and as the composer of Greensleeves.

IRON AGE (c700BC - c100BC) A period in European history which began with the manufacture of iron weapons and implements - as opposed to Bronze - and ended with the Romans. In Britain, this period was marked by distinctive hill forts and a pastoral economy.

JAMES VI & I, KING OF SCOTLAND (1567 - 1625) KING OF GREAT BRITAIN (1603 - 1625) b. 1566 Became King at a very tender age when his mother, Mary, Queen of Scots (qv), was forced to abdicate. His father, Darnley having been murdered with his mother's connivance, James was left in the care of a variety of Scottish nobles. A shrewd and flexible diplomat, James managed to tame the wilder excesses of his nobles and keep the church in check too.

Hailed as a great King of Scotland, his reputation as a king in England after his accession to the throne was decidedly dodgy. He was seen as a drunken, foul mouthed, undignified coward with homosexual leanings. His financial irresponsibility, pro Spanish foreign policy and continuous assertions of royal authority led to a deterioration of relations between Parliament and the monarchy which led ultimately to the execution of his son, Charles I.

JEFFRIES, JUDGE. Following Monmouth's 1685 rebellion against James II, Chief Justice Jeffries presided over a large number of assize courts (known as the Bloody Assizes) where over 1,000 rebels were brutally treated. This did not endear him, or the king, to the general populace.

JOHN, KING OF ENGLAND (1199 - 1216 b. 1167) Younger brother of Richard the Lionheart he was Regent in his brother's absence. Not content with succeeding to the throne of England, he renewed the war with France and lost most of the English possessions there. His objections to the Pope's nomination for Archbishop of Canterbury led to his excommunication in 1212. His objections to the power of his barons led to Magna Carta (qv) in 1215. Not so much the monster portrayed by history as a weak and stubborn man, with a cruel streak.

JOSEPH OF ARIMATHAEA, SAINT (Dates uncertain) Asked Pontius Pilate for the body of Christ following the Cruxifiction and arranged for His burial. Medieval legend brings him to Glastonbury with the Holy Grail and building the first Christian

Church there. Other legends suggest that he may have brought Christ to Glastonbury as a boy.

KIPLING RUDYARD (1835 -1936) Nobel prize winning author of The Jungle Books and many other well-loved stories and poems.

MAGNA CARTA (1215) Drawn up by a number of barons to curb the power of King John (qv), it is often mistakenly seen as a civil rights charter for the common people. The baron's would never have shot themselves in the foot in that way.

MARSTON MOOR, BATTLE OF (1644) Yet another indecisive battle during the Civil Wars (qv). It effectively destroyed the King's hold on Northern England, but the Roundheads did not follow up their victory to truly turn the tide in their favour.

MARY, QUEEN OF SCOTS (1542 - 1587). Three times married mother of James VI & I (qv), she is often implicated in the plot which led to the murder of her second husband, Darnley, through the agency of her third, James Hepburn, Earl of Bothwell. She was a constant thorn in the side of her cousin, Elizabeth I (qv) who eventually gained sufficient evidence to convince her that Mary was attempting to become Queen of England and had her executed.

MATILDA, THE EMPRESS (1102 - 1167) Unpopular granddaughter of William the Conqueror, she was rejected as Queen of England in favour of her cousin Stephen (qv) against whom she fought a desultory civil war. Had the last laugh when Stephen was forced to accept her son (later Henry II) as his heir.

MCGONAGALL, WILLIAM (1830 - 1902) Could be known as The Awful Rhymer. McGonagall, during his lifetime - was just about the only person who thought he was a poet. Has something of a cult following today.

MESOLITHIC AGE (c 12,000BC - 5,000BC) Middle period of the Stone Ages which began at the end of the last ice age and ended - for Britain - when we literally parted company with mainland Europe.

PENDRAGON, UTHER (Dates & existence uncertain) According to legend, Uther was father to King Arthur (qv) another character whose dates & existence are uncertain. Vaguely associated with Tintagel in Cornwall. May have been modelled on Ambrosius Aurelianus to give Arthur street-cred.

PILGRIMAGE OF GRACE (1536). An essentially peaceful uprising - or rather series of uprisings - in the North of England against the dissolution of the monasteries and in support of the Catholic church. Led by Robert Aske, 35,000 men marched on Doncaster where they were met by Henry VIII's (qv) emissary, the Duke of Norfolk. Talks were held and the men dispersed. Further minor uprisings in 1537 led to severe repression and the execution of Robert Aske.

PLANTAGENETS. A dynasty of British monarchs descended from the Empress Matilda (qv) and her second (French) husband, Geoffrey Plantagenet, Count of Anjou. The name is derived from the Latin Planta Genista, the common broom, which was the family emblem. Last of the line was Richard III.

PRESTON, BATTLE OF (1715) Not much fighting, not often considered worthy of the title battle, usually known as The Surrender. Jacobite forces under Thomas Forster and the Earl of Derwentwater capitulated and thus ended much chance of the Old Pretender sitting on the English Throne.

REFORMATION Name given to the changeover from Catholicism to Protestantism. Hastened in England by Henry VIII's desire to marry Anne Boleyn and the Pope's intranstigency in refusing a divorce from Katherine of Aragon.

RESTORATION (1660) England became a monarchy again under Charles II. (See Civil Wars)

RICHARD II (1377 - 1399. Born 1367) Began as a successful king, probably under the guidance of his uncle, John of Gaunt. Lost control for a while to the 'Merciless Parliament'. Later became tyrannical, banishing Henry Bolingbroke (later King Henry IV) among other apparently senseless acts. Was probably murdered in Pontefract Castle.

RICHARD III (1483 - 1485. Born 1452) Gained fame, but never popularity, as a soldier whilst his brother, Edward IV (qv) was king. Shakespeare (qv) has him portrayed as a hunchbacked monster, responsible for the murder of the Princes in the Tower. There is no evidence that he was hunchbacked, but it was certainly politically expedient for Henry VII to have him maligned.

ROSES, WARS OF THE (1455-1487) This is perhaps a rather grandiose title for intermittent fighting, lasting no more than 13 weeks in total, during which the crown of England changed hands 6 times. It began during the reign of Henry VI, whilst he was mentally incapable of ruling. Control was sought by the Lancastrian, or Court Party under Henry's wife, Margaret of Anjou supported by the Beauforts and the Yorkists led by Richard, Duke of York. They ended when the Lancastrian claimant to the throne, Henry VII married the eldest daughter of Edward IV (qv) a Yorkist king.

ROUNDHEADS Derogatory name for the Parliamentarian soldiers during the Civil Wars (qv).

RUSKIN, JOHN (1819 - 1900) Artist, writer, lecturer, critic and traveller extraordinary, Ruskin was the first Slade Professor of Fine Art at Oxford.

SHAKESPEARE, WILLIAM (1564 - 1616) England's finest playwright and a role model for Goebbels. His character assassination of Richard III - by fingering him for the murder of his nephews, the Princes in the Tower - was as superb a job as ever done by modern propagandists. For hundreds of years his version of the events following the death of Edward IV were publicly accepted and taught in schools as the truth. His Tudor paymasters were rightly proud of him.

SOUTHEY, ROBERT (1774 - 1843) Brother-in-law of Coleridge and friend of William Wordsworth (qv). Often - erroneously - classed as a Lakeland Romantic poet, Southey was more of an historian. His poems - mostly ballads and epics - are more reminiscent of an earlier era.

STANWICK, BATTLE OF (79) The Roman General Agricola was on the rampage, subduing native Britons whenever and wherever possible. At Stanwick in Teesdale he massively defeated a Brigantian fortress under the command of Venutius. Thereafter the Brigantes resorted to guerilla warfare.

STEPHEN, KING OF ENGLAND (1135 - 1154, b. 1100). Grandson of William the Conqueror who fought a desultory civil war for the crown of England against his cousin Matilda (daughter of the previous king, Henry I and granddaughter of William the Conqueror). Upon the death of his only son in 1153, Stephen was forced to name Matilda's son, the future Henry II as his successor.

TOWTON, BATTLE OF (1461) Decisive defeat of Lancastrians in a snowstorm left Edward IV (qv) undisputed King of England during the Wars of the Roses (qv).

TURNER, JOSEPH MALLORD WILLIAM (1775 - 1851) English landscape artist much preoccupied with the effects of light and colour.

WAKEFIELD, BATTLE OF (1460) A rare defeat for Richard of York - later Richard III (qv) - during the Wars of the Roses (qv).

WORDSWORTH, WILLIAM (1770 -1850) Romantic poet & republican, friend of Coleridge - whom some suspect to have been his inspiration - and Poet Laureate. He's best remembered for his lines about daffodils.

WORLD WAR, FIRST (1914 - 1918) Also known as the Great War and The War to End All Wars (it didn't). The British Empire, France, Russia, Belgium, Japan, Serbia, Italy, Portugal, Romania, Greece and the USA versus Germany, the Austro-Hungarian Empire, Bulgaria and Turkey. The longer list won.

VICTORIA, QUEEN OF ENGLAND, EMPRESS OF INDIA (1837 - 1901. Born 1819) Granddaughter of George III, she inherited the throne from her uncle, William IV. Married her cousin Albert and bore him 9 children. Her popularity took a tumble when she shut herself away from the public for ten years after Albert's early death. May or may not have had a close relationship with John Brown, her Scottish gillie.

Additional Acknowledgements

The Text

The author wishes to thank librarians and archivists at :

Boston Mass, Bradford, Carlisle, Chester, Darlington, Freemantle WA, Hull, Kendal, Lancaster, Leeds, Liverpool, Northallerton, Richmond, Ripon, Savannah Geo, Sedbergh and York.

And individuals, too numerous to mention, for access to personal collections and family documents.

The Pictures

The grey scale pictures were derived from 35 mm colour transparencies taken by the author. They have been image processed from Kodak CD by Maureen Ann Kristen using Corel Photo-Paint.